Perceptions of the Independence of Judges in Europe

Frans van Dijk

Perceptions of the Independence of Judges in Europe

Congruence of Society and Judiciary

palgrave
macmillan

Frans van Dijk
Faculty of Law, Economics and Organization
Utrecht University
Utrecht, The Netherlands

ISBN 978-3-030-63142-0 ISBN 978-3-030-63143-7 (eBook)
https://doi.org/10.1007/978-3-030-63143-7

This Palgrave Macmillan imprint is published by the registered company Springer Nature Switzerland AG
The registered company address is: Gewerbestrasse 11, 6330 Cham, Switzerland

Preface

This book is about the perception of the independence of the judiciary in Europe. Do citizens and judges see it in the same way? Do judges feel that their independence is respected by the users of the courts, by the leadership of the courts and by politicians? Does the population trust the judiciary more than other public institutions, or less? How does independence of the judiciary work at the national level and at the level of the European Union? These interrelated questions are particularly relevant in times when the independence of the judiciary is under political pressure in several countries in the European Union. The judiciary may not have direct democratic legitimacy, but how the judiciary and its core value, independence, are perceived in society is still—or even more so—important. At the end of the day, these perceptions determine popular support of the judiciary in society, and thereby its position in the trias politica.

Surveys among judges, lay judges and lawyers—in addition to regular surveys among the general public organized by the European Commission—provide a wealth of information to answer all of these questions. The surveys were conducted by the European Network of Councils for the Judiciary (ENCJ), encompassing all countries that participated in its work, whether or not these countries have councils for the judiciary. The surveys are a part of the ENCJ's efforts to improve independence and accountability of the judiciaries of Europe, by setting standards and measuring the realization of these standards, as well as measuring independence and accountability in general. The survey among lawyers was organized together with the Council of Bars and Law Societies of Europe (CCBE).

These instruments were developed in a project I coordinated, on behalf of The Netherlands Council for the Judiciary. At that time, I was director of The Netherlands Council. This book was not commissioned by the ENCJ and does not necessarily reflect the opinion of the ENCJ, and neither does it reflect the opinion of The Netherlands Council for the Judiciary. I wrote this book in my capacity as professor of Empirical Analysis of Legal Systems at the Montaigne Centre for Rule of Law and Administration of Justice of Utrecht University. The book combines the outcomes of the surveys that have been conducted in this field. Its approach is primarily descriptive. It presents descriptive statistics, and occasionally some linear regressions, primarily for the purpose of illustration. I hope the analysis presented here is accessible to a broad audience. This is a first step, and further research is needed into the underlying mechanisms of the formation of perceptions of judicial independence.

I would like to thank the colleagues from the judiciaries of Europe that participated in the development and execution of the ENCJ-surveys, and in particular past and present presidents of the ENCJ, Geoffrey Vos, Nuria Diaz Abad, Kees Sterk and Filippo Donati, and the director of the ENCJ, Monique van der Goes. The survey among lay judges was made possible by Wiggo Storhaug Larssen. I would like to thank Sarah Koolen, in particular, for doing much of the organizational work on the surveys. Chapter 4 of this book contains joint work with Bart Diephuis and Frank van Tulder of The Netherlands Council for the Judiciary. I would like to thank Bart Diephuis for additional statistical analyses. And finally, I would like to thank the ENCJ and the Montaigne Centre for covering the costs of open access.

Utrecht, The Netherlands — Frans van Dijk

Contents

1 Introduction 1

2 Judicial Independence and Perceptions of Judicial Independence 7

3 Perceptions of Judicial Independence in European Countries 29

4 Perceptions of Lay Judges About Independence of the Judiciary 53

5 Respect for Judicial Independence 65

6 Independence and Trust 77

7 Judiciary in Democracy: Alignment and Disconnect 93

Index 111

List of Figures

Fig. 3.1	Perceived judicial independence by public and judges, average per country	37
Fig. 3.2	Perceived independence by the general public, by level of education, average per country	38
Fig. 3.3	Score of judicial independence by the public and by companies, without and with experience with disputes in court, average for 22 countries and average scores for Italy and for Czechia	45
Fig. 5.1	Respect of independence of the judiciary by parties to judicial proceedings and parliament, average per country	73
Fig. 6.1	Trust of citizens in national and EU institutions, percentage of respondents that tends to trust, average per country	90
Fig. 7.1	Alignment of judiciary and society, average scores per country	99

List of Tables

Table 2.1	Overview of perceptions and comparisons (arrows) that are presented	24
Table 3.1	Surveys on judicial independence by category of respondents	30
Table 3.2	Summary statistics of the perceptions of judicial independence by judges (own independence and independence of all judges), lawyers, general public and companies, for countries of Europe	32
Table 3.3	Summary statistics of the perceptions of judicial independence by judges and lawyers and by citizens and companies with and without experience, for 17 countries of Europe	33
Table 4.1	Setting in which lay judges adjudicate cases: number of answers given by type of setting, as percentage of total answers	55
Table 4.2	Summary statistics of the perceptions of judicial independence of lay judges by lay judges (personally and all lay judges) and professional judges by lay judges, the perceptions of independence of professional judges (personal and general) by professional judges and the perceptions of independence by the general public, for 10 judiciaries	57
Table 4.3	Determinants of perceived independence of lay judges, linear regression	60

Table 5.1	Respect for independence as perceived by judges by categories of actors, for 24 countries of Europe	69
Table 5.2	Determinants of respect for independence by selected actors as perceived by judges, linear regression	71
Table 6.1	Pearson correlations of the perception of independence of and trust in the judiciary for 25 countries	79
Table 6.2	Summary statistics of trust of the general public in the state powers and the press for 25 countries	81
Table 6.3	Summary statistics of trust of the general public in the public sector for 25 countries	84
Table 6.4	Summary statistics of trust of the general public in National and EU institutions across 25 countries	88
Table 6.5	Pearson correlations of independence and respect for independence as perceived by judges and independence and trust perceived by citizens	91
Table 7.1	Trust, perceived independence and respect for independence for three groups of countries	97

CHAPTER 1

Introduction

Abstract The central question that this book will try to answer is whether there is a lack of alignment and—in the extreme—a disconnect between the judiciary and society in countries of Europe (EU and UK). This central question is developed into six sub questions. The sub questions focus on perceptions of judicial independence by various actors, their respect for independence and the trust of the general public in the judiciary.

Keywords Judicial independence · Perceptions · Trust

No state can do without a judiciary, but that does not mean that the judiciary is aligned with the population and appreciated by it. It is generally believed that a high degree of judicial independence is necessary for people to appreciate and trust the courts. After all, the fair and effective resolution of disputes requires an independent and impartial adjudicator, irrespective of the parties and interests involved. In turn, trust is seen as necessary for courts to be able to function, if only to incite people to bring their disputes to court, to cooperate with the court and to accept judgments willingly. The causal relationship between judicial independence, trust and reliance on the courts puts sharp focus on judicial independence as it is perceived by the population and all segments thereof. Courts

F. van Dijk, *Perceptions of the Independence of Judges in Europe*,
https://doi.org/10.1007/978-3-030-63143-7_1

may be fully independent, but if the population does not recognize this independence, the causal relationship is disrupted.

At the same time, it must be recognized that judiciaries are under pressure from many sides, whether from parties and lawyers or media and politics. In particular when judgments are feared not to turn out the desired outcome, litigants—whether or not they subscribe to the need for independence in general—have an incentive to try and influence court decisions in their favour. They do so appropriately, but also inappropriately, the latter to the detriment of independence. Governments or parliaments may not want to surrender important decisions to review by an independent judiciary, and may attempt to keep some level of control over the courts. There are many ways to inappropriately influence the judiciary, and ultimately its judgments might be ignored.

The relative vulnerability of the judiciary in withstanding pressure and fulfilling its role has been stressed often. The classic reference is to Hamilton, who argued that the judiciary is the weakest of the three state powers: judges only make decisions in disputes that are put to them, and the judiciary itself does not implement or enforce the decisions (Hamilton 2009 [1788]). In addition, the judiciary's functioning can be frustrated by the other state powers in many ways, for instance by reducing access to the courts by raising legal or financial barriers, by reducing the funding of the judiciary and by exploiting their role in appointments of judges and members of governing bodies such as councils for the judiciary. The other state powers have the practical means to make or break the judiciary. The degree of respect for the independence of the judiciary by relevant private and public actors is therefore an important factor for the level of independence in a concrete situation. An actor's respect for independence reflects the legitimacy of the judiciary, but also the willingness of this actor to support the rule of law, even when it is not in his or her direct interest.

Independence of the courts, in combination with the permanent threats to undermine it, requires judiciaries to be organized separately from public and private interests, and in particular from the other branches of the state. This necessary separation creates an autonomous environment with strong professional culture and traditions, expressed in professional and ethical standards. The downside is the risk of lack of alignment and even a disconnect with society. Judges who are complacent among themselves, may miss incentives to connect with parties and to keep up with society.

Lack of alignment will show in different perceptions of independence by judges and other groups in society. Of course, perceptions will always differ among the general public and diverse groups such as companies, court users, lawyers and judges, given their different roles, experience and culture. Alignment is, therefore, a matter of degree. It should also be recognized that the perceptions of independence by the general public are influenced by other factors than direct experience. Reporting in the media and political discourse play a role as well. For instance, in the shift in some countries in Eastern Europe towards an authoritarian state or a—so called—illiberal democracy, the independence of the judiciary functions as a barrier, leading to concerted efforts of governments and state controlled media to discredit the judiciary among the population. The larger the lack of alignment between judges and citizens, the easier it becomes for governments to curtail the independence of the judiciary and to diminish the rule of law, but also the more difficult the daily functioning of the courts becomes.

Is lack of alignment a real problem? When asked, the judges of Europe evaluate the independence of the judges in their country positively. On a scale of 0 to 10, averages per country range from a moderate 6.5 in Latvia to a very high 9.8 in Denmark, with an average across countries of 8.5 for 25 countries in 2019 (all these and other figures mentioned in this introduction will be discussed in later chapters). So, judges do not perceive a lack of independence. If you ask lawyers for their opinion, however, their assessment of the independence of the judiciary is substantially less positive. That is the conclusion in all countries that took part in both the lawyers survey and the survey among professional judges. The range is between 5.2 in Hungary to 9.0 in the UK with an average of 6.7, considerably lower than the average of the judges. The Eurobarometer survey among citizens shows even lower scores than the ones given by lawyers. The Eurobarometer range is between 3.7 and 7.3, with an average of 5.4. Apart from the question which perceptions are closer to 'real' (de facto) independence, these findings point to different perspectives of judges and society. Lack of alignment seems apparent between the two.

Weak alignment is also manifest in the extent judges say their independence is respected by the other state powers, government and parliament, and by the media and social media. A broad variation exists among the member states of the EU, with negative extremes—unsurprisingly—in Poland (72% of the judges did not feel respected by the government and

62% by the media in 2017), but also in Romania (58 and 53% in 2019) and the UK (43 and 52% in 2019).

It could be argued that these findings are not very important, when trust in the judiciary among the general public is high. Whatever the merit of this argument, this proves not to be the case. Firstly, the opinion of citizens about judicial independence is closely connected with their trust in the justice system. This is reflected in the correlation between trust and perceived independence, as will be discussed. In essence, trust in the judiciary seems to equal trust in the independence of the judiciary. Secondly, the percentage of respondents that tend to trust the justice/legal system varies widely from 17% in Croatia to 86% in Finland, with a cross country average of 52% in June 2019, according to a regular public opinion survey of the European Commission. Trust is an issue in many countries. On the positive side, in most countries trust in the judiciary is higher than that in government and parliament. Across countries, the difference between trust in the judiciary and each of the two other powers is close to 15% point. Lack of alignment with society is not only an issue for the judiciary, but also for government and parliament.

How do we interpret these findings? Multiple explanations of the differences in perceived independence are possible. In one scenario, judges are complacent and over-confident about their independence, and the assessments of the other groups reflect the true state of independence more accurately. The perception of many judges of lack of respect by the other state powers, could then be a reflection of over-accentuating the role of the judiciary in society. In this scenario, the judiciary is inward-looking and self-protective, a closed community that sets its own standards. In another scenario, opinions of citizens and business and to some extent lawyers are unavoidably shaped by the fact that most court cases have winners and losers. Losses are accentuated, and blamed on judges that are thought not to be impartial and independent. Opinion in society is affected by critical reporting of such and other cases by the (social) media, in some countries in combination with or driven by negative opinions of governments and parliaments that do not subscribe to current constitutional principles and may not want to abide with these principles. In this scenario, the judiciary performs well within the context provided by the other state powers, but this is not recognized by the population.

To explore the relative merit of these two scenarios, this book discusses perceptions of independence, respect for independence and trust, in the countries of the EU and the UK. The **central question** is addressed **whether there is in Europe a lack of alignment and—in the extreme—a disconnect of judiciary and society and, if so, what causes this**. This is primarily done by analysing the data from surveys. This analysis is made possible by the recent surveys of the European Network of Councils of the Judiciary among (lay) judges and in co-operation with the Council of Bars and Law Societies of Europe (CCBE) among lawyers in Europe. This data is combined with the outcomes of surveys of the European Commission among the general public and among companies. To answer the central question, the following sub-questions are addressed for the countries that are covered by the surveys.

1. How do the perceptions of judicial independence by judges, lawyers, court users and citizens and companies compare? As to the general public and companies, a follow-up question is whether characteristics of the respondents play a role. Taking into account the limited availability of data about the parties in court procedures, how do these parties experience independence? (Chapter 3)
2. Can the perceptions of lay judges who as citizens have direct experience at the bench, and bridge the gap between judges and society, throw light on the factors that determine the perceptions of citizens? In particular, how do professional and lay judges interact, and how does this affect perceptions? (Chapter 4)
3. How do judges experience the respect for their independence by the categories of actors they interact with: (1) court users: parties, lawyers and prosecutors, (2) the political system, consisting of government, parliament and the (social) media and (3) the internal leadership of the judiciary, provided by the highest courts and by the governance institutions of the judiciary? (Chapter 5)
4. Given the relationship between perceived independence and trust in the judiciary by the public and given the generally higher trust in the judiciary than in the other state powers, how can this differential trust be understood? Does the multi-level governance structure of the EU, also with respect to the judiciary, play a role? (Chapter 6).
5. In view of all data, can it be concluded that a lack of alignment and, in the extreme, a disconnect exists between judiciary and society, in the European Union in general and/or in specific countries? And what can be concluded about its causes and effects? Are there

indications of the stability of the equilibrium of the state powers? (Chapter 7)
6. Have these findings implications for the functioning of the judiciary in a democracy? (Chapter 7)

To set the scene, Chapter 2 discusses the main theoretical and empirical findings in the literature pertinent to these issues, and their implications for the design of this study.

This study has limitations. The most important limitation is the lack of differentiation of respondents in the surveys used. It is likely that citizens with different social and cultural backgrounds experience judicial procedures differently and also perceive judicial independence differently. Especially, court user surveys could throw more light on these differences in the future. Another limitation is the focus on descriptive statistics, as there is a wealth of data to present and analyse. The implication is that to a large extent explanation and causality have to left to a later occasion.

Reference

Hamilton, A. 2009 [1788]. The judiciary department. Federalist 78. In *The Federalist Papers*. Palgrave Macmillan.

CHAPTER 2

Judicial Independence and Perceptions of Judicial Independence

Abstract The three key concepts of this study are: perceived judicial independence, respect for judicial independence and trust in the judiciary. To provide the basis for the empirical chapters that follow, theoretical considerations are explored. Due to the subjective nature of independence, perceptions matter. According to European case law, the appearance of independence needs to be taken into account when the independence of a court is evaluated. The perceptions held by parties, lawyers, media, general public and judges are not homogeneous, and depend on different sets of factors. In the literature, it is widely believed that the judiciary needs a positive perception of independence to gain the trust of society. This trust in turn bolsters the legitimacy of the judiciary. Trust and legitimacy are many-faceted concepts. In this study trust is used in the sense of diffuse institutional trust. Respect for independence is used as an expression of the legitimacy of the judiciary. These concepts apply to the national courts and to the courts at the EU/European level. To understand judicial independence in Europe, both levels need to be examined in conjunction.

Keywords Judicial independence · Impartiality · Trust · Respect · Multilevel governance

F. van Dijk, *Perceptions of the Independence of Judges in Europe*,
https://doi.org/10.1007/978-3-030-63143-7_2

2.1 Relevance of Perceptions of Judicial Independence

Independence is the core principle and value of the judiciary and also its performance yardstick. This is expressed in many basic documents. Focusing on Europe, Article 6(1) ECHR states that "in the determination of his civil rights and obligations or of any criminal charge against him, everyone is entitled to a fair and public hearing within a reasonable time by an independent and impartial tribunal established by law". As the current president of the Court of Justice of the European Union puts it succinctly, "… the principle of judicial independence constitutes the essence of the fundamental right to effective judicial protection" (Lenaerts 2020, p. 32). This function of independence follows from the division of power among the branches of the state to protect citizens in disputes with the state. However, the emphasis on independence also derives from the raison d'être of the judiciary to adjudicate any dispute fairly, in a predominantly confrontational setting. The courts take far reaching decisions about people and their lives. Parties—often very unequal in resources and power—disagree and quarrel, often in a highly charged and emotional atmosphere. To put it simply, they want to win (or at least not lose), and are often willing to go to extremes to achieve this. This confrontational aspect distinguishes the judiciary from most other professional organizations, and puts the independence of the judge at the forefront. A judge cannot be an effective arbitrator if she is not independent and impartial, and is seen as such by the parties.

Independence is a multi-faceted phenomenon. The case law of the highest European courts, the Court of Justice of the European Union and European Court of Human Rights, give insight in what is seen as particularly important. According to the Court of Justice: "… in order to establish whether a tribunal is 'independent' within the meaning of Article 6(1) of the ECHR, regard must be had, inter alia, to the mode of appointment of its members and their term of office, the existence of guarantees against outside pressures and the question whether the body at issue presents an appearance of independence…".[1] While this statement does not constitute a definition of independence or a full description of relevant factors, it provides a useful insight into what is currently on top of

[1] CJEU, Combined Cases C-585/18, C-624/18 and C-625/18, ECLI:EU:C:2019:982, Judgment of 19 November 2019, para. 127.

the mind of leading justices. Appearances is one of them. This statement also reflects different concepts of independence. The aim of the Court of Justice is to establish the actual independence of a court in a specific case. To do this it singles out the mode of appointment of judges and the existence of guarantees of independence. These aspects are part of, what is often called, the de iure independence of the judiciary: the formal arrangements that shape and protect the independence of the judiciary. There are many more aspects of de iure independence than mentioned here (see for instance the indicator system of the ENCJ for an exhaustive list [ENCJ 2020]). The Court also refers to the appearance of independence. How parties and others perceive the independence of the judge(s) in the case at hand is important. The Court of Justice has set a high standard: regarding guarantees rules should be set "in order to dispel any reasonable doubt in the minds of individuals as to the imperviousness of that body to external factors and its neutrality with respect to the interests before it."[2]

The prominent role of perceptions reflects the difficulties for those involved in procedures to establish in a straightforward manner whether or not judges are independent. Ideally, one would like to establish 'objectively' the actual independence of judges as it shows in their behaviour and decisions: in judges' behaviour in court (how they conduct hearings) and, in particular, in their judgments. These judgments should 'prove' the extent to which they are being led only by the law, and to this end are 'impervious' to inappropriate external (political and private) pressures and internal pressures (from other judges and management). This is for several reasons, apart from the technical nature of legal issues, difficult to do. Being led only by the law means that political, religious or other background does not play a role in adjudicating cases. While background may not play a large role in most run-of-the mill cases (Ashenfelter et al. 1995), it becomes an issue in controversial cases. The Chief Justice of the US in his reply to criticism of the President of that country on alleged political bias of a judge who ruled against a migrant asylum order of the President, expresses this aspiration clearly: "We do not have Obama judges or Trump judges, Bush judges or Clinton judges. What we have is an extraordinary group of dedicated judges doing their level best to

[2] CJEU, Case C-216/18, ECLI:EU:C:2018:586, Judgment of 25 July 2018, para. 66.

do equal right to those appearing before them".[3] This goal puts high demands on the way judges are selected and promoted: selection needs to be based on merit (knowledge and experience), and not on other (such as political) considerations. However well this selection is done, reality is that judgments reflect values anyway. The extent to which judges are able and willing to abstract from their convictions and their backgrounds is an empirical question but hard to research, let only be established in the heat of the court case by the court users in anything close to objectivity.

The second aspect, being impervious to pressure, is equally subjective. It is made complicated by the qualifier 'inappropriate'. If it comes to corruption in its diverse forms, it is by definition that this is inappropriate pressure (including temptation), and the relevance of safeguards against such outside pressure is evident. Otherwise, there will always be pressure for instance by the media, and undergoing pressure—appropriate and inappropriate—from all sides and withstanding it, is part of being a judge. This resilience is to be achieved not by judges isolating themselves from society, as they are expected to be in touch with society (Warner et al. 2014). How else can a judge know how deeds that come before the bench affected society? When external pressure becomes inappropriate is arbitrary and subjective. Similarly, internal pressures on judges may come from a court president who puts pressure on a judge to decide a case in a certain way, but the court president may also enquire about the delay in a court case or from colleagues who together agree on a guideline for the penalty for a certain type of crime. Again, what is inappropriate is arbitrary and subjective.

Given these and other inherently subjective aspects, it is relevant how judicial independence is perceived in individual court cases as stipulated in the reasoning of the Court of Justice, but it is also relevant at an aggregate level to evaluate the independence of the judiciary as a whole. Systematic measurement is needed for this purpose not only of the perceptions of the parties, but also of the perceptions of other categories such as lawyers, media, general public as well as judges themselves. The perceptions of a variety of actors are relevant in particular because they see different parts of reality, have different interests and stakes, and are likely to be subject to different biases.

[3] Roberts as quoted by AP, 22 November 2018.

Perceptions of judges are, for instance, informative about the pressures they are under, but may be less so to capture whether they are influenced by their beliefs. The perceptions of parties and lawyers are directly relevant, but their perspectives may be heavily influenced by (expected) outcomes, while the perceptions of the media are similarly relevant, but may be biased towards sensationalist reporting. The perceptions of the general public are likely to be diffuse, but in a democracy essential to understand the role given to the judiciary in society.

2.1.1 Independence and Impartiality

Independence and impartiality are often used in combination. The already quoted Art 6(1) ECHR offers an example. The two terms are used next to each other, and the relationship between the two needs to be clarified here. While independence refers to a general state of mind but also to institutional arrangements, impartiality relates to the state of mind of the court (the judge) towards the issues and parties in a case (OHCHR 2003). No prejudice, preference or bias is to be expressed in any way at hearings or otherwise. As for independence, the case law of the Court of Justice gives an indication what impartiality entails in the view of the court:

> ... impartiality can, according to equally settled case-law of the European Court of Human Rights, be tested in various ways, namely, according to a subjective test where regard must be had to the personal convictions and behaviour of a particular judge, that is, by examining whether the judge gave any indication of personal prejudice or bias in a given case; and also according to an objective test, that is to say by ascertaining whether the tribunal itself and, among other aspects, its composition, offered sufficient guarantees to exclude any legitimate doubt in respect of its impartiality. As to the objective test, it must be determined whether, quite apart from the judge's conduct, there are ascertainable facts which may raise doubts as to his or her impartiality. In this connection, even appearances may be of a certain importance.[4]

[4] CJEU, Combined Cases C-585/18, C-624/18 and C-625/18, ECLI:EU:C:2019:982, Judgment of 19 November 2019, para 128.

The Court of Justice attaches importance to appearances, like with independence. Independence and impartiality are closely linked and overlapping concepts. It is assumed here that the independence of the judge in a case is a necessary but not sufficient condition for her impartiality in that case. It is questionable whether the parties can recognize whether a judge is independent. It is more likely that parties can recognize whether a judge is impartial or not. Impartiality is then an imperfect indicator of independence. In existing court user surveys in as far as these surveys address such fundamental matters (which they normally do not), the relevant question is about impartiality (Netherlands, US) or neutrality (Denmark).

2.2 Formation of Perceptions of Independence

The formation of perceptions of judicial independence varies among categories of actors. Delivering justice differs from receiving justice, and direct personal experience differs from indirect information through social networks or the media. To start with the parties, according to the extensive literature on procedural justice the neutrality of the decision maker is one of four key aspects that determine the fairness of a procedure, the others being voice, respect and trustworthiness (see the review of Tyler and Sevier 2013/2014). Thus, the independence and impartiality of the judge are an integral part of the procedural justice attained by the courts (also, Grootelaars and van den Bos 2018; CEPEJ 2016). Ideally, procedures are conducted in such a way that also the losing parties are satisfied with the fairness of the procedure. While they may not agree with the outcome, they accept the judicial decisions, implement them voluntarily and support the courts (Tyler and Sevier 2013/2014). The expectation would be that, if procedural fairness is realized to a high degree, the satisfaction with the court among the parties that the court ruled in favour of and among the parties it ruled against would not differ much. This would then also be the case for perceptions of independence.

Reality is often different. With fair procedures, it may be possible to achieve—but it is by no means guaranteed—that both parties appreciate the interaction as fair, and evaluate the experience as positive, irrespective of winning or losing. This positive experience would lead to an improvement of sentiments among the parties and positive sentiments towards the court. In other situations, the interaction will be evaluated negatively by the losing party, strengthening the negative sentiments about the other party and creating negative sentiments about the court.[5] This extends to the perception of independence. In addition, when parties lose their case, they or their lawyers are tempted to rationalize the loss by assuming that the judge was partial and not really independent. 'Justice must be seen to be done', but do losing parties recognize justice when it is done? A survey among court users in the Netherlands shows significant differences between winners and losers with respect to their experience, even if in both groups most respondents are positive about the experience.[6,7] As losing weighs heavier than winning (Kahneman and Tversky 1984) and in general negative events weigh heavier than positive events (Baumeister et al. 2001), it is not assured that what is expressed in surveys is a true representation of judicial independence. A negative bias is more likely. While lawyers are partisan as well, they will be less emotionally involved than the parties, have realistic expectations about what to expect and by being a lawyer are less put off by complex, formalistic legalities. Their perspective could therefore be less biased.

As to perceptions among the general public, most citizens have infrequent contact with the courts (see Sect. 3.5). As most people do not have recent, direct personal experience with the courts, the experiences and beliefs of those who have such experiences, translate into public opinion about the independence of the judiciary by means of interpersonal networks, reporting on social and traditional media and through the political arena. In the traditional media and social media negative experiences with the courts are likely to be accentuated. This holds for all media but in particular for what may be called sensationalist media (Johnston and Bartels 2010). Politicians may react to critical opinions of aggrieved court users, especially when re-enforced by the media. They may also have their own agendas with regard to democracy and the balance of the state powers, which may or may not respect each other's role. The (dis)respect shown by relevant actors for the independence of the judiciary is likely

[5] See van Dijk et al. (2002) on the development of positive and negative sentiments as a result of social interaction.

[6] Parties for whom the judgement is (expected to be) favourable are significantly more often positive about the performance of the judiciary than parties seeking justice for whom the judgement is (expected to be) unfavourable: respectively, 90% and 62% are (very) satisfied and 3% and 14% are (very) dissatisfied (Regioplan and Ipsos 2015).

[7] The CEPEJ 2016 model questionnaire includes for court users a question whether the court found in favour of the court user concerned (CEPEJ 2016).

to affect public opinion. While it is the duty of all governmental and other institutions to respect and observe the independence of the judiciary (OHCHR 1985), in reality otherwise can be observed. An example for the United States was already given. In Europe Poland is a particular case in point (i.a. Venice Commission 2020). Thus, the perceptions of the general public about the independence of the judiciary are an amalgam of influences. It should be stressed that the perceptions of the general public are particularly relevant as these inform decisions of individuals to bring cases to court, to refrain from legal action or, if available, to use other methods of dispute resolution. These perceptions will also play a role in political decisions about the legal system. Given the function of the courts in economic interaction, the views within the business sector are similarly relevant.

Finally, the judges themselves. They have not (or are not supposed to have) a vested interest in court cases like the parties and lawyers. They have first-hand experience with the practical implementation of formal guarantees of independence, the actual pressures (and temptations) on judges from outside and inside the courts, but also how judges personally or as a group react to pressure. The downside is, of course, that they have to evaluate themselves and their colleagues, and, while judges are trained to be cool observers, whether they can do that when it concerns themselves or their group is another matter.

To conclude, the perceptions of the categories of stakeholders that were discussed, are formed by very different mechanisms. As a consequence, their perceptions have different characteristics and biases, and their combination is necessary to construct a full picture. Together the perceptions can shed light on the elusive 'de facto' independence of the judiciary. In addition, actors that bridge boundaries are of particularly relevance here. In Chapter 4 the perceptions of lay judges are discussed.

2.3 Independence, Trust and Legitimacy

There is a widespread understanding supported by empirical evidence that independence is necessary for the judiciary to gain the confidence of society and that a high level of confidence bolsters the legitimacy of the judiciary in the sense of its licence to operate. Confidence and legitimacy are seen as essential for the courts to fulfil their function. In the judgment of the Court of Justice of the European Union that was already cited about independence in Sect. 2.1, the court continues: "…

it being added, in that connection, that what is at stake is the confidence which such tribunals must inspire in the public in a democratic society." And similarly with regard to impartiality: "Once again, what is at stake is the confidence which the courts in a democratic society must inspire in the public, and first and foremost in the parties to the proceedings". In the same vein, Lenaerts sees independence and impartiality as necessary for court rulings to enjoy authority and legitimacy (Lenaerts 2020, p. 31). In these wordings independence and impartiality are instrumental to achieve the confidence in and authority and legitimacy of the courts. This is strongly felt by others in the field as well, to such an extent that it has become a common understanding. It also adds another aspect to the importance of independence as perceived in society. Before we look into these causal relationships, we need to discuss briefly the different concepts used in the literature and their meaning.

2.3.1 *Trust and Legitimacy*

Trust, legitimacy and related concepts apply to public institutions in general, but have also been examined with specific reference to the courts. As Hamm et al. (2011) notes, in the literature about the judiciary in its connection with society terms like confidence, trust, trustworthiness, public support, loyalty, legitimacy and felt obligation to obey the law as well as negatively charged notions like scepticism, cynicism and distrust are used. These diffuse concepts are often used interchangeably but they are sometimes defined distinctly. Also, in the vast literature on trust a variety of types of trust is distinguished, such as dispositional trust (as a basic individual attitude), interpersonal trust, institutional trust—in diffuse form (trust in an institution in general) and specific form (trust in an institution to do something specific such as uphold the law)—and political trust. To complicate matters, the trust of a person in an institution may be evolving, depending on information and experience gained. For instance in the case of the judiciary, if a person has no experience with the courts or even with government in general, the person will exhibit his dispositional trust when asked whether he trusts the courts. Once he has experiences with the public sector, dispositional trust will be replaced by institutional trust that he will apply to the courts as well. After concrete experience with the courts, diffuse and specific trust in the courts may take over (Mayer et al. 2006). Linguistically, some of these concepts do not travel well: for instance confidence and trust translate into the same term in German and Dutch (an easy check is to compare the cited case law in different languages as available at the website of the CJEU). Relevant in the current context is also that trust can be defined as perceived trustworthiness of somebody or an institution, but can also be seen to relate to trusting behaviour. The latter involves giving up power to another over outcomes that are important for oneself. In this approach trust is more than a passive evaluation without obligation. This interpretation applies in particular to the interpersonal level (Tanis and Postmes 2005), but it is also relevant for trust in the courts. This is obviously the case when deciding to go to court: one gives up willingly or unwillingly control over one's situation (see Benesh 2006). A person puts his fate in the hands of the court, and expects that it gets fair treatment. Finally, trust is also sometimes used in the sense that an actor is trusted to behave in a certain way (Mayoral 2017): the actor behaves as expected, for instance by doing what is in his (narrow) self-interest.

The Court of Justice uses, as the quote before shows, the term confidence in the courts. Confidence is also used in much research about the US (GBAO 2020; Benesh 2006; Hamm et al. 2011). Public opinion surveys by the EC use the term trust (EC 2020b). Also in view of the linguistic issues, trust in the courts and confidence in the courts are used interchangeably here.

Trusting behaviour in the courts is close to other concepts such as felt obligation to obey the law (Hamm et al. 2011), but also, more recently, to respect for the independence of the courts (ENCJ 2019). Both concepts are related to institutional legitimacy and the public's compliance with institutions (Tyler and Sevier 2013/2014). Felt obligation to obey is either seen as part of legitimacy or as an outcome of legitimacy (Tyler and Huo 2002; Tyler and Jackson 2014; Gibson and Caldeira 1998). In an experimental study among students, Hamm et al. (2011) finds separable effects on overall confidence in the courts in general of dispositional trust, trust in institutions, obligation to obey the law and cynicism. In the following the terms trust/confidence, in the sense of diffuse trust, and respect for judicial independence as a consequence of institutional (judicial) legitimacy are used. It is unfortunate that surveys that focus on negative concepts such as cynicism are currently not available for Europe, as such data would provide a valuable complement (Tyler and Huo 2002).

While the surveys about independence and respect for independence among judges, lay judges and lawyers have been developed by the ENCJ recently, with regard to trust recourse has to be taken to existing opinion surveys, and the questions as phrased in these surveys, have to be accepted. For instance, the opinion survey of the European Commission asks: "Do you tend to trust the judicial/legal system?" This phrase leaves very much open. Do respondents answer the question whether courts are trustworthy or whether they are willing to relinquish control by bringing their disputes to court? Given the limited experience of citizens with the courts, answers are also likely to reflect a combination of dispositional trust, trust in government in general and trust in the courts.

2.3.2 *Empirical Relationship Between Independence and Trust*

The connection between independence on the one hand and confidence or trust on the other hand can now be considered. It was already noted that it is the clear view of the Court of Justice of the European Union that independence as well as impartiality lead to confidence in the courts. Empirical studies confirm the connection between independence and confidence. Benesh (2006) in a key study about the State Courts in the US, based on a survey by the National Center for State Courts, hypothesizes that procedural justice, implying a fair arbiter, as well as the institutional design of the courts related to independence affect confidence, in addition to type of experience (party or juror). In the American context institutional design concerns whether judges are appointed or elected. The hypothesis is that elected judges who have to campaign for election are less independent than appointed judges. Both hypotheses (procedural justice and independence) hold. Cann and Yates (2008) finds that judicial elections and judicial campaign contributions undermine support for the US state courts. Support is measured by among other perceptions of the trustworthiness of judges and whether decisions are perceived to be based on facts and law. Citizens are concerned about costly, partisan election campaigns. Cann and Yates finds that more independence leads to higher confidence. It finds also that citizen characteristics, race and gender and social capital, play a role. Intriguingly, greater knowledge of the legal system reduces the perception of court legitimacy. The study suggest that a realistic view on the functioning of the court leads to a less positive perception, and confidence evolves into a more instrumental opinion based on specific outcomes.

Buhlmann and Kunz (2011) examines the impact of the independence of the judiciary on the confidence of citizens in the justice system by means of a multi-level analysis for a range of countries, using data from diverse sources. The study finds that the perceptions of judicial independence in society are formed by actual (de facto) independence and not (directly) by the formal rules and safeguards that protect the independence of the judiciary, de iure independence, and that these perceptions foster confidence in the judicial system. Contrary to expectations, it also finds that political and economic 'winners' have greater confidence in the judiciary than 'losers', irrespective of degree of independence. The study suggests that independence gives judges the opportunity to decide matters according to their ideological views or in an arbitrary way, but other explanations are conceivable. For instance, 'winning' and 'losing' may be related to level of education. In the next Chapter the impact of education on perceptions of independence is examined. It has been suggested furthermore that there is a causal relationship between the existence of impartial institutions in a broad sense and generalized (dispositional) trust, but the evidence is not conclusive (Rothstein and Stolle 2008).

More specifically, Sapignoli (2018) uses the Eurobarometer public opinion surveys of the EU to find that the perceived independence of magistrates is strongly correlated with the trust of citizens in the judicial system, and even more so than the effectiveness of the judicial system in guaranteeing the rule of law. These opinion surveys will be examined in Chapter 6. Finally, experimentally the relationship between impartiality as part of procedural justice and trust has been established (Grootelaar and van den Bos 2018). As discussed before, independence and impartiality are closely connected.

To conclude, trust in the judiciary seems to be equal to trust in the independence of the judiciary. While independence is particularly relevant for the judiciary (but not only for the judiciary, see below), trust in the judiciary can be compared with that in the other state powers (Chapter 6).

Having established the link between independence and trust, the statement of the Court of Justice, quoted earlier, requires further attention. Its underlying premise is that the judiciary needs the trust of the population to be able to function. Why is it necessary for the judiciary to be trusted? Is this trust functional and does it add anything to the perception of independence? This seems a rather trivial question, but the reasoning is of some interest. While the importance of trust holds true for the other powers of the state as well in a democracy, for the judiciary this is often seen as particularly important. The main arguments are well known: (1) as mentioned earlier, in most fields of law parties have a choice to bring their disputes to court, do nothing or pursue different courses of action, and, once having gone to court and having received judicial decisions, the enforcement of the judgments is external to the judiciary, and (partly) depends on parties accepting the authority of the courts (Tyler and Sevier 2013/2014). This applies to criminal law as well: trust affects willingness to report crimes and for witnesses to cooperate with the police (Tyler and Huo 2002; Warner et al. 2014). Also, the acceptance of judgements in general, even when unpopular, is greater when diffuse support is higher (Gibson et al. 2005). (2) Lacking direct democratic legitimation and being dependent on the other state powers in many respects for instance for funding, the judiciary is vulnerable to encroachment by the other state powers (Cann and Yates 2008; Rehnquist 2000; Langer 2002). Attacking an institution that is trusted widely, may undermine one's own position, and thus backfire.

While both arguments raise complications which will be discussed in Chapter 7, the essence that the courts need trust to function, is not contested in the literature. It is, however, an open question how this works in practice.

2.4 Behaviour of the Judiciary to Enhance Independence

The second argument (position in trias politica) reverses the relationship between trust and independence. A judiciary that is trusted in society, stands a better chance to get—wholeheartedly or grudgingly—from politics the independence it existentially needs to function or it is more immune to attempts of infringement. The judiciary therefore has an incentive to build trust, in as far as this is within its powers. Given the link with independence, this is not necessarily doing what people think is desirable, such as heavier sentences for crimes always and everywhere. The choice judiciaries face is to build either diffuse or specific support. It has been shown in a study for the Netherlands that citizens feel that sentences are too lenient, but that they also think that judges should be independent, and should decide at they do (de Keyser et al. 2007). Thus, society wants judicial independence, and that is what is trusted.

This chain of effects from building trust in the judiciary among the general public to strong support in government and parliament for the judiciary is not trivial, especially given the decentralized and non-hierarchical nature of the judiciary. What may work for the public, may not necessarily work in politics. These processes are not only occurring with regard to the judiciary. The public sector has seen a—what is called—agencification (Papadopoulos 2013). Traditional government bureaucracies have been replaced by single-purpose organizations that implement specific laws and regulations. These agencies have a high degree of autonomy or even independence to shield them from partisan political influence. The development of the literature in political science about these autonomous agencies is of interest here. A major review of this literature identifies as an important trend increased attention for agency autonomy as 'a dynamic, relational and socially constructed phenomenon' (Verhoest 2017). In this approach autonomy, reputation and trust are linked. It suggests that agencies can gain more autonomy or defend their autonomy by developing a strong reputation with relevant actors and by creating a strong network of support for the agency.

This thinking applies to the judiciary as well, while recognizing that independence is more fundamental for the functioning of the judiciary than autonomy is for agencies. Obviously, the actual independence of the courts is not a static characteristic of a legal system (de iure independence), as the cases of Poland and Hungary graphically show (e.g. Coman 2014; Kovács and Scheppele 2018). Strong legal foundations of independence can be lost in the course of a few years. The case of Poland in particular highlights that legal safeguards do not always offer protection, as relevant laws have been changed relatively easily and rapidly there. Following the reasoning of this political science literature, protection does not come from existing laws or even the constitution, but from excellent performance for the court users and active policies to build support. The trust and reputation of the judiciary are then aspects that strengthen or weaken the position of the judiciary. While active networking would also be effective, in the judiciary this meets often with resistance, as courts keep and treasure their distance from other organisations, just to protect their independence. Still, bar associations and civil society are often natural allies. However, with these constraints on networking and lobbying, building trust and support of the general public seems to be particularly important for the judiciary.

These arguments strengthen the relevance of the subject matter of this book, as perceptions about the judiciary in society may play an even more crucial role than laws and formal safeguards. An open question is whether judiciaries are looking at their position in this way. Do they have governance structures that allow them to work on their reputation consciously and in a co-ordinated manner or can the same results be achieved by synchronized behaviour of individual judges? These issues are beyond this book.

2.4.1 Multi-level Governance

In his review Verhoest (2017) emphasizes that the relational aspect of autonomy also concerns the multi-level governance structure within the EU. National political decision makers have to take into account the policies of the EU. As Braithwaite and Drahos (2000) put it, nations are rule-takers rather than rule-makers. Multi-level governance is obviously relevant for the judiciary in view of the presence of courts at the European level, to which was referred already several times. In the EU legal order, the hierarchy of institutions, if it is appropriate to use this term, is stronger with regard to the courts than with regard to the other state powers, in as far as the mandate of the EU is concerned and it is uncontested. National judges are also European judges and national courts are decentralized courts, applying EU law and European standards. National judges ask for guidance of the Court of Justice of the European Union. In the case of Poland about the independence of the judiciary, the influence exerted by institutions at the European level on national institutions is particularly observable, where the European Court of Justice and the European Court of Human Rights play an important role next to the political institutions of the EU (Kovács and Scheppele 2018). This case is an illustration of the interaction of levels of governance: the Court of Justice intervenes directly in national policies and legislation, and instructs the authorities to take measures. At the end of the day, however, if countries do not abide by its decisions, the court depends on the European Commission in particular to enforce its judgments. The EC promotes and tries to maintain the independence of national judiciaries and the stability of the division of powers in all member states. The Justice Scoreboard of the EC is an example of a monitoring mechanism (EC 2020a). Given this structure, the interaction mechanism suggested above repeats itself at the EU-level. Independence, trust, legitimacy and respect for independence all play a role. The trust of the national populations in the EU institutions and the perceptions about the independence of the Court of Justice of the European Union and European Court of Human Rights are relevant for the functioning of the whole multi-level system.

The EU level adds a dimension to the independence of and trust in the judiciary, as national judges have opinions about the independence of the EU-courts and have a degree of trust in them, and vice versa. Also, national judges have views about the independence of judges in other member states and their trustworthiness. These issues have been dealt with by others (Mayoral 2017), but also need more data to be gathered. The focus here is on the actual alignment or lack of alignment of judiciary and society in Europe, as basis for the judiciary to fulfil its mandate to provide effective protection of rights using the terminology of the Court of Justice.

2.5 Alignment of Judiciary and Society

Judicial independence is still often seen as stemming from the formal arrangements in law and constitution, and as static as long as the legal provisions remain the same. However, legal provisions are subject to change, and need to be stabilized, if one wants to maintain them as they are. The independence of the judiciary is permanently constructed by the behaviours of many actors, and is inherently dynamic. The simplified scheme below captures the main concepts. While trust and legitimacy may be empirically hard to distinguish, there is a case to be made to distinguish them. One can trust the judiciary fully, and still be of the opinion that the judiciary lacks legitimacy, in particular democratic legitimacy. Also, the judiciary may have democratic legitimacy, for instance by means of election of judges, but this may affect, as discussed above, perceived independence negatively, and this impacts trust negatively as well.

Perceived judicial independence	↔	Trust in judiciary
↕		↕
Respect of judicial independence	↔	Legitimacy of the judiciary

The main causal direction is probably clockwise, but causality also runs the other way, as discussed in the previous section. A major issue is whether the system that is represented by the scheme, is in equilibrium.

Equilibrium may arise out of virtuous and negative cycles. How equilibria would look like, and what their stability is, is a huge subject in itself. In Chapter 7, this subject will be briefly discussed.

It must be emphasized that all four concepts are likely to be specific for categories of actors. Respect for judicial independence is a clear case in point. Respect is likely to differ among categories of actors, such as the court users (parties and their lawyers, prosecutors), the political system (parliament, government and the media), but also actors within the judiciary (supreme court, court management and councils for the judiciary). These categories have different involvements with the judiciary and different interests and motivations. While for politicians respect for independence ideally means no interference with the judiciary, proper implementation of judicial decisions, seeing to it that the resources of the judiciary are adequate and reluctance to criticize the judiciary, and for the media substantive, factual reporting of court cases and refraining from personal attacks (such as 'enemies of the people'), for parties, lawyers and prosecutors it would mean not to resort to inappropriate behaviours (attempts to bribe judges, threaten judges), but to implement judicial decisions if there is the choice not to do so, and to exert democratic rights to support the judiciary. Within the judiciary itself, respect would mean for court management and councils for the judiciary not to put pressure on judges to adjudicate cases, for instance, from an efficiency point of view. This reasoning applies to all four concepts of the scheme. However, the availability of data is a limiting factor. Table 2.1 gives the differentiation that is applied in the next Chapters.

Another aspect of the data is from which perspective perceptions are measured. One can ask, for instance, citizens about their perceptions of judicial independence, but one can also ask judges how they think citizens perceive judicial independence. Taking the perspective of the behavioural reactions of the judiciary as in previous sections, the perceptions of judges of how society perceives its independence and whether relevant groups in society respect judicial independence are particularly relevant. However, perceptions about perceptions become quickly complicated. In this book all data are based on first order surveys, except for respect for judicial independence. It does not make much sense to ask people whether they respect the independence of the judiciary if one wants to avoid socially desirable answers, but it makes sense to ask judges whether they feel their independence is respected, as they experience this directly in the courts. This leads also to some complications, as will be discussed in Chapter 5.

Table 2.1 Overview of perceptions and comparisons (arrows) that are presented

	National institutions	EU institutions
Perceived judicial independence	Perceptions of: • General public • Companies • Lawyers • Judges • Lay judges • Parties	
Perceived respect of independence	Respect of judicial independence, as perceived by judges, by: • Parliament • Government • Media • Judicial institutions • Lawyers • Parties	
Trust	Trust by general public in: • Courts • Parliament • Government • Other public institutions	Trust by general public in: • Court of Justice of the European Union • European Parliament • European Commission

The differentiation of categories of stakeholders is an essential part of this study. The alignment of judiciary and society shows not only in the extent society in a broad sense is convinced of the independence of the judiciary and trusts its judiciary, but also in the extent that the perceptions of the functioning of the judiciary among judges and (groups in) society differ. The relevance of differences in perceptions of judges and the (potential) users of the courts in a broad sense comes to the fore in particular when judges are much more positive than society about their performance. Such differences feed the feeling in society that judges are otherworldly, live in an ivory tower and are protective of their position. To be satisfied about oneself, while the court users are unhappy, is likely to have negative consequences for trust. In addition, perceptions drive behaviour, causing a tendency not to see a need for change within the judiciary, where others outside the judiciary see this need as urgent. See Rottman and Tomkins (1999) which notes for the US state courts a large difference in the appreciation of the functioning of the courts between population and judges with judges not seeing a need for change. Finally and as a consequence, differences may create tensions and strife among the state powers. Large (unexplained) differences in perceptions of judicial independence may tempt the other branches to intervene or to strengthen their grip on the judiciary. In the next Chapters, while filling in Table 2.1, the focus will be on differences.

References

Ashenfelter, O., T. Eisenberg, and S.J. Schwab. 1995. Politics and the judiciary: The influence of judicial background on case outcomes. *Journal of Legal Studies* 24 (2): 257–281.

Baumeister, R.F., E. Bratslavsky, C. Finkenauer, and K.D. Vohs. 2001. Bad is stronger than good. *Review of General Psychology* 5 (4): 323–370.

Benesh, S.C. 2006. Understanding public confidence in American courts. *Journal of Politics* 68 (3): 697–707.

Braithwaite, J., and P. Drahos. 2000. *Global business regulation*. Cambridge: Cambridge University Press.

Buhlmann, M., and R. Kunz. 2011. Confidence in the judiciary: Comparing the independence and legitimacy of judicial systems. *West European Politics* 34 (2): 317–345.

Cann, D.M., and J. Yates. 2008. Homegrown institutional legitimacy; Assessing citizens' diffuse support for State Courts. *American Politics Research* 36 (2): 297–329.

CEPEJ. 2016. Handbook for conducting satisfaction surveys aimed at court users in Council of Europe member states, 2018 edition (2016 data). https://rm.coe.int/168074816f.

Coman, R. 2014. Quo vadis judicial reform? The quest for judicial independence in Central and Eastern Europe. *Europe-Asia Studies* 66 (6): 892–924.

de Keijser, J., P. van Koppen, and H. Elffers. 2007. Bridging the gap between judges and the public? A multi-method study. *Journal of Experimental Criminology* 3: 131–161.

ENCJ. 2019. Independence and accountability of the judiciary: ENCJ Survey on the independence of judges 2019. encj.eu.

ENCJ. 2020. Independence, accountability and quality of the judiciary: Measuring for improvement. ENCJ Report 2019–2020. encj.eu.

European Commission. 2020a. 2020 EU Justice Scoreboard.

European Commission. 2020b. Eurobarometer Interactive, Public opinion survey. https://ec.europa.eu/commfrontoffice/publicopinion/index.cfm/Chart/index.

GBAO. 2020. State of the State Courts, Survey analysis.

Gibson, J.L., and G. Caldeira. 1998. Changes in the legitimacy of the European Court of Justice: A post-Maastricht analysis. *British Journal of Political Science* 28: 63–91.

Gibson, J.L., G. Caldeira, and L.K. Spence. 2005. Why do people accept public policies they oppose? Testing legitimacy theory with a survey-based experiment. *Political Research Quarterly* 58: 187–201.

Grootelaar, H.A.M., and K. van den Bos. 2018. How litigants in Dutch courtrooms come to trust judges: The role of perceived procedural Justice, outcome favorability, and other sociolegal moderators. *Law and Society Review* 52 (1): 234–267.

Hamm, J.A., L.M. PytlikZillig, A.J. Tomkins, M.N. Herian, B.H. Bornstein, and E.M. Neeley. 2011. Exploring seperable components of institutional confidence. *Behavioral Sciences & the Law* 29: 95–115.

Johnston, C.D., and B.L. Bartels. 2010. Sensationalism and sobriety; Differential media exposure and attitudes toward American courts. *Public Opinion Quarterly* 74 (2): 260–285.

Kahneman, D., and A. Tversky. 1984. Choices, values, and frames. *American Psychologist* 39: 341–350.

Kovács, K., and K. Scheppele. 2018. The fragility of an independent judiciary: Lessons from Hungary and Poland—And the European Union. *Communist and Post-Communist Studies* 51: 189–200.

Langer, L. 2002. *Judicial review in state supreme courts: A comparative study*. Albany: State University of New York Press.

Lenaerts, K. 2020. New horizons for the rule of law within the EU. *German Law Review* 21: 29–34.

Mayer, R.C., J.H. Davis, and F.D. Schoorman. 2006. An integrative model of organizational trust. In *Organizational trust: A reader*, ed. R.M. Kramer, 82–108. New York: Oxford University Press.

Mayoral, J.A. 2017. Impact through trust: the CJEU as trust-enhancing institution. iCourts Working Paper 105.

OHCHR. 1985. Basic principles on the independence of the judiciary. https://www.ohchr.org/EN/ProfessionalInterest/Pages/IndependenceJudiciary.aspx.

OHCHR. 2003. Human rights in the administration of justice: A manual on human rights for judges, prosecutors and lawyers.

Papadopoulos, Y. 2013. *Democracy in crisis? Politics, Governance and Policy*. Cham: Palgrave Macmillan.

Regioplan and Ipsos. 2015. Klantwaardering Rechtspraak 2014.

Rehnquist, W.H. 2000. Reflections on the history and future of the Supreme Court of the United States. Speech at the D.C. Circuit Judicial Conference.

Rothstein, B., and D. Stolle. 2008. The state and social capital: An institutional theory of generalized trust. *Comparative Politics* 40 (4): 441–459.

Rottman, D.B., and A.J. Tomkins. 1999. Public trust and confidence in the courts: What public opinion surveys mean to judges. *Court Review* 36 (3): 24–31.

Sapignoli, M. 2018. Trust in justice in EU countries: Level of support and correlated factors. Paper prepared for 2018 EGPA Conference, Study Group XVIII on Justice and Court Administration.

Tanis, M., and T. Postmes. 2005. A social identity approach to trust: interpersonal perception, group membership and trusting behaviour. *European Journal of Social Psychology* 35: 413–424.

Tyler, T.R., and J. Sevier. 2013/2014. How do the courts create popular legitimacy? The role of establishing the truth, punishing justly and/or acting through just procedures. *Albany Law Review* 77(3): 1095–1137.

Tyler, T.R., and Y.J. Huo. 2002. *Trust in the law: Encouraging public cooperation with the police and the courts*. New York: Russell-Sage Foundation.

Tyler, T.R., and J. Jackson. 2014. Popular legitimacy and the exercise of legal authority: Motivating compliance, cooperation, and engagement. *Psychology, Public Policy, and Law* 20: 78–95.

van Dijk, F., J. Sonnemans, and F. van Winden. 2002. Social ties in a public good experiment. *Journal of Public Economics* 85: 275–299.

Venice Commission. 2020. Poland, Joint urgent opinion of the Venice Commission and the Directorate General of Human Rights and Rule of Law of the Council of Europe, Opinion No. 977/2019.

Verhoest, K. 2017. Agentification. In *The Palgrave Handbook of Public Administration and Management in Europe*, ed. E. Ongaro and S. van Thiel, 327–346. Basingstoke: Palgrave Macmillan.

Warner, K., J. Davis, M. Walter, and C. Spiranovic. 2014. Are judges out of touch? *Current Issues in Criminal Justice* 25 (3): 729–744.

CHAPTER 3

Perceptions of Judicial Independence in European Countries

Abstract The perceptions of judicial independence of judges, lawyers, general public and companies are analysed across countries. The perceptions of these categories are strongly correlated. However, the mean scores differ: judges are much more positive about their independence than lawyers, and lawyers are much more positive than the general public and companies. As to the general public, highly educated citizens are generally more positive about the presence of independence than citizens with lower education levels. The difference increases with the degree of independence. Citizens with little education in very different countries have similar perceptions of judicial independence. The limited information that is available about court users suggests that persons with recent experience with the courts are less positive about independence than persons without experience. For companies the reverse is apparent. Among both the general public and companies, the perceptions diverge more with experience than without experience, likely as a result of winning or losing a case.

Keywords Judicial independence · Survey · Judges · Lawyers · Citizens · Court users

F. van Dijk, *Perceptions of the Independence of Judges in Europe*,
https://doi.org/10.1007/978-3-030-63143-7_3

3.1 Surveys About Independence

Several surveys about judicial independence are available for countries of Europe. Table 3.1 provides an overview. These surveys allow a comparison of the perceptions of citizens and companies in general with the perceptions of lawyers and judges. In this Chapter these perceptions are compared and analysed. Since 2016 surveys are conducted at the request of the European Commission annually about the perceptions of judicial independence among the general public and among companies. The European Network of Councils for the Judiciary (ENCJ) has held by now three surveys among the judges of Europe about their independence. The latest survey was conducted in February/March 2019. The surveys

Table 3.1 Surveys on judicial independence by category of respondents

	Number of respondents	*Country coverage*	*Period of collection*	*Terminology in relevant question*
General public	26,446	28 EU-members	January 2019	Courts and judges
Companies	6,808	28 EU-members	January 2019	Courts and judges
Court users (parties)	1,573 (citizens) 734 (companies)	As the above surveys	January 2019	Courts and judges
	Varied	Some national surveys	Misc.	Judge
Lawyers	4,489	21 Countries with sufficient response	1 Qtr 2019	Judge
Judges	11,335	27 ENCJ members and observers, incl. Norway, from 25 countries	1 Qtr 2019	Judge
Lay judges	20,605	10 ENCJ members and observers	1 Qtr 2018	Judge

Note The UK participated in all surveys, and is included in the comparisons

Sources

General public: Flash Eurobarometer 474 (EC 2019b)

Companies: Flash Eurobarometer 475 (EC 2019a)

Parties: Flash Eurobarometer 474 and 475 and miscellaneous national surveys

Lawyers: ENCJ and CCBE (2019)

Judges: ENCJ (2019)

Lay judges: ENCJ (2018)

are aimed at professional judges. A separate survey has been carried out by the ENCJ among lay judges in 2018. The opinions of lay judges are the subject of the next Chapter. As to the perceptions of lawyers, at the initiative of the ENCJ the Council of Bars and Law Societies of Europe (CCBE) has recently organized—in parallel with the latest judges survey—a survey among lawyers in 2019. The participation of lawyers in the survey was relatively low and for some countries too low to be informative, despite the efforts of national bar associations. Given the crucial role of lawyers in judicial procedures, this is unfortunate, but together with the other data sources a consistent picture can be constructed.

Then, there are the court users for whom the judicial system exists, but who are difficult to reach. Some information about their perceptions can be derived from the surveys mentioned above at the request of the EC among citizens and companies, as these contain a question about their recent involvement in a dispute that went to court. However, people do not go to court often, and the number of respondents per country is small, while EU-wide aggregate data are not very meaningful given the differences among the constituent nations. In addition, only for a few countries relevant data on the perceptions of court users about concepts that are related to independence are available, as part of court user surveys. Court user surveys generally focus on the services provided by the courts at a practical level, and pay attention to issues such as waiting times, but in some surveys court users were asked about impartiality (the Netherlands) and neutrality of the judge (Denmark).

It should be noted that the comparison of the perspectives of the stakeholders in the judiciary can also be done for an individual country. An example is an interesting study regarding Montenegro that distinguishes the same stakeholders as in this Chapter, and involved extensive data collection (World Bank 2018).

Table 3.2 summarizes the key outcomes of the surveys. As the country coverage of the surveys does not fully overlap, a full comparison is possible for 17 countries (left part of the Table). Leaving out the perceptions of lawyers, 22 countries can be compared (right part). In the notes to the Table the countries in the two sets are specified. It should be noted that of the large countries of the EU France and Poland did not participate in the 2019 judges survey of the ENCJ. France, because of administrative reasons, and Poland, because it has been suspended as a member of the ENCJ (2019). Table 3.2 does not include the court users in the sense

Table 3.2 Summary statistics of the perceptions of judicial independence by judges (own independence and independence of all judges), lawyers, general public and companies, for countries of Europe

	N = *17*					N = *22*			
	Judges own	*Judges all*	*Lawyers*	*Public*	*Companies*	*Judges own*	*Judges all*	*Public*	*Companies*
Mean	8.9	8.2	6.7	5.4	5.5	8.9	8.2	5.5	5.6
Min–Max	7.1–9.3	6.5–9.4	5.2–9.0	3.7–7.3	3.2–7.3	7.1–9.8	6.6–9.8	2.6–8.0	2.5–8.6
SD	0.6	0.8	1.1	1.1	1.3	0.6	0.9	1.4	1.6
Countries with large differences among categories									
Italy	9.3	8.4	6.6	4.4	3.9				
Slovakia	9.1	8.1	5.4	3.7	3.2				
Countries with small differences among categories									
Latvia	7.1	6.5	6.2	5.0	4.9				
Germany	8.9	8.6	7.0	6.9	6.7				
Sweden	9.1	8.6	8.2	7.3	7.3				
Correlation									
Judges own	1	0.86**	0.41	0.32	0.27	1	0.88**	0.57**	0.52*
Judges all		1	0.75**	0.62**	0.58*		1	0.80**	0.75**
Lawyers			1	0.76**	0.72**	×	×	×	×
public				1	0.90**			1	0.94**
Companies					1				1

Notes

1. Judges and lawyers: score on a scale of 0–10, where 0 is no independence at all and 10 is maximally independent. Public and companies: 5 point scale, transformed linearly to 11-point scale

2. All correlations are at country level. Significance levels: *0.05 and **0.01

3. Paired sample T-test of means at country level: all means differ significantly (<0.01), except public and companies for both sets of countries

4. 17 judiciaries: BE, CZ, DE, EL, ES, IE, IT, HU, LT, LV, NL, PT, RO, SK, SI, SW, UK

22 judiciaries: AT, BE, BG, CZ, DE, DK, EL, ES, IE, IT, FI, HR, HU, LT, LV, NL, PT, RO, SK, SI, SW, UK

For abbreviations see list at the end of the chapter

Table 3.3 Summary statistics of the perceptions of judicial independence by judges and lawyers and by citizens and companies with and without experience, for 17 countries of Europe

	Judges all	*Lawyers*	*Public*		*Companies*	
			Experience	*No experience*	*Experience*	*No experience*
Mean	8.2	6.7	5.0	5.5	5.7	5.4
Min–Max	6.5–9.4	5.2–9.0	3.5–7.3	3.5–7.3	2.4–8.7	3.2–7.3
SD	0.8	1.1	1.0	1.1	1.9	1.4
Correlation						
Judges all	1	0.75**	0.54*	0.61**	0.76**	0.50[1]
Lawyers		1	0.60**	0.76**	0.77**	0.68**
Public with experience			1	0.79**	0.71**	0.80**
Public no experience				1	0.74**	0.95**
Companies with experience					1	0.76**
Companies no experience						1

[1] $p = 0.051$

Note Paired sample *T*-test of means on country level: the means regarding judges and lawyers differ significantly (<0.01) from the means of public and companies. The means regarding the public with and without experience differ significantly (<0.05). The other means regarding companies and between public and companies do not differ significantly (>0.05)

of the parties in procedures, because their experience requires a more nuanced description (see Table 3.3). The perceptions of the different actors, starting with the judges, are discussed in the following.

3.2 Independence as Perceived by Judges

The judges of Europe are generally positive about their independence. The ENCJ survey asked judges of 27 countries to rate their own independence as well as the independence of the judges in general in their country.[1] The first question has a personal and narrow scope. The mean score over all 27 judiciaries was 9.0 on an 11-points scale from 0 to 10.

[1] Literally: "On a scale of 0-10 (where 0 means "not independent at all" and 10 means "highest possible degree of independence") as a judge I am ...". Same, but: "the professional judges in my country are ...".

49% of the respondents gave their independence the maximum score of 10 and 28% a score of 9.[2] Only 4% gave a score lower than 6. The question about the independence of the judges in general is less personal as well as potentially broader, as respondents may take aspects such as the selection of judges into account. The mean score was lower, 8.3 with 'only' 24% of the respondents awarding a score of 10 and 31% 9. Just above 7% gives a score lower than 6. Looking at the outcomes per country, the mean scores on own independence range from 7.1 in Latvia to 9.8 in Denmark and on the independence of the judges of the country from 6.5 in Latvia to again 9.8 in Denmark.

The correlation between the scores on the two questions is high. They differ systematically in level, nevertheless. The difference between the mean scores on own independence and on independence of all judges increases with the decrease of the mean score for all judges.[3] This can be explained partly by the existence of an upper bound which limits the possibilities to score one's own independence when the score for all judges is already close to the ceiling. Another reason might be unwillingness to express lack of independence at the personal level, for instance for fear of negative consequences if the guaranteed anonymity of the survey would be breached.[4] Still, it seems that it is not beyond judges to be susceptible to illusory superiority (Buunk and Van Yperen 1991), which for instance brings nearly all people to think that they drive their cars better than the median (Svenson 1981), and also offers an explanation why lawsuits go to trial (Landes 1971; Posner 1973). While there are many explanations of this phenomenon, the outcome is likely to be influenced by the context of self with aggregate comparison (Giladi and Klar 2002). Being critical about colleagues may have to do with the actual observation of colleagues in court and their judgments, but also with the appointment and promotion of judges. The ENCJ survey shows that many judges are critical about human resource decisions about judges, and many respond that these decisions are not solely based on merit (see ENCJ 2019, p. 33).

[2] Average of countries, to avoid influence of country size.

[3] Linear regression at country level: Ind All = 1.4**× Ind Own − 4.3**, $N = 26$, $R^2 = 0.76$. Thus, if Ind Own = 10, Ind All = 9.7, and if Ind Own = 8, Ind All = 6.9. Note: excluding Northern Ireland.

[4] Respondents were given a link to the ENCJ website, administered in Brussels.

In view of these explanations, the score for all judges is likely to be a more truthful expression of actual independence than the score for one's own independence. In addition, Table 3.2 shows that the judges' perceptions about judges in general are more strongly correlated with the perceptions of lawyers, citizens and companies than the perceptions of judges about themselves. In the remainder the perceptions about all judges will be used as yardstick for the opinion of judges. It should be stressed that this yardstick concerns the independence of the judiciary, and not the perception of judges of the appearance of independence to the parties and the public. The question of the survey is explicitly phrased in this way.

3.3 Independence as Perceived by Lawyers

The survey among lawyers about the independence of the judiciary in their country includes exactly the same question as the survey among the judges about the independence of the judges in general. Lawyers are much more critical about judicial independence than the judges themselves. The mean score over the 17 countries with sufficient response rates is 6.7 with 10% of the respondents giving a score of 10 and 16% a score of 9. 31% allots a score below 6. At country level, the average score ranges from 5.2 for Hungary to 9.0 for the UK.

The left part of Table 3.2 allows a comparison of lawyers and judges. The perceptions of judges about the independence of the judges in general in their country are highly correlated with the perceptions of the lawyers, while the means differ substantially. This essentially implies that the surveys reveal very similar, consistent differences of perceptions between countries, but they also bring out different views about the level of independence that is achieved.

The mean score by lawyers across countries of 6.7 can be seen as positive, but much less so than the mean score by judges of 8.2. The lower the score given by lawyers, the larger is the difference between the mean score by judges and the mean score by lawyers.[5] Compare for instance Hungary and Sweden. For Hungary the score of judicial independence by judges is 7.3 and the score by lawyers is 5.2, resulting in a large difference. For Sweden the scores are 8.6 and 8.2. This phenomenon is similar to that with regard to the two types of perceptions of judges discussed

[5] Linear regression at country level: Ind All Judges = −0.5** × Ind Lawyers + 4.8**, $N = 17$, $R^2 = 0.53$. If Ind Lawyers = 5, Ind All Judges = 7.3. If Ind Lawyers = 8, Ind All Judges = 8.8.

above. While admittedly lawyers form a critical profession, it is not likely that as a personality trait they are inherently more critical/negative in Hungary than in Sweden. The only exception of the pattern is Latvia. The scores of judges and lawyers are very similar (6.5 vs 6.2). Evaluating the data at individual level for Latvia, reveals that there is no significant difference between judges and lawyers. For each of the other countries the difference is significant.[6]

3.4 Independence as Perceived by the General Public

Perceptions of the general public are derived from a survey that is fully devoted to the topic of judicial independence. The Eurobarometer phrases the question as follows: "from what you know, how would you rate the justice system in (y)our country in terms of the independence of the courts and judges? Would you say it is very good, fairly good, fairly bad or very bad", allowing also "do not know" as an answer. While the wording and the scale differ, the content is the same as that of the surveys among judges and lawyers. After transformation to an 11-point scale, the mean outcome for all 22 members is 5.5 with a range of 2.6 for Croatia to 8.0 for Denmark.[7] Table 3.2 gives the scores for the two subsets that are used to compare the categories of actors. Comparing the perceptions of judges (about all judges), lawyers and the public, the mean score drops from 8.2 to 6.7 and to 5.4: lawyers are more critical about judicial independence than judges, and the general public is more critical than the lawyers. For some countries this pattern does not affect the (positive) perception of independence qualitatively (see Fig. 3.1). In these countries all categories of actors are positive about the state of independence (score >5), albeit to a larger or smaller degree. This is the case for instance for the Netherlands, Sweden and the UK. For other countries the outcomes diverge. For instance, in Spain the score by the judges is 7.8, by lawyers 6.2 and by the public 4.2. This pattern is also found in Slovenia and Italy. This puts in doubt the state of independence in these countries:

[6] T-test. Significance level: 0.1% for all countries except Sweden (1%) and UK (5%). For Latvia $p = 0.18$.

[7] A simple linear transformation was used to transform the five points scale of the EU barometers as follows: very good: 10, fairly good: 7.5, don't know: 5, fairly bad: 2.5 and very bad: 0. Alternative transformations do not alter the outcomes qualitatively.

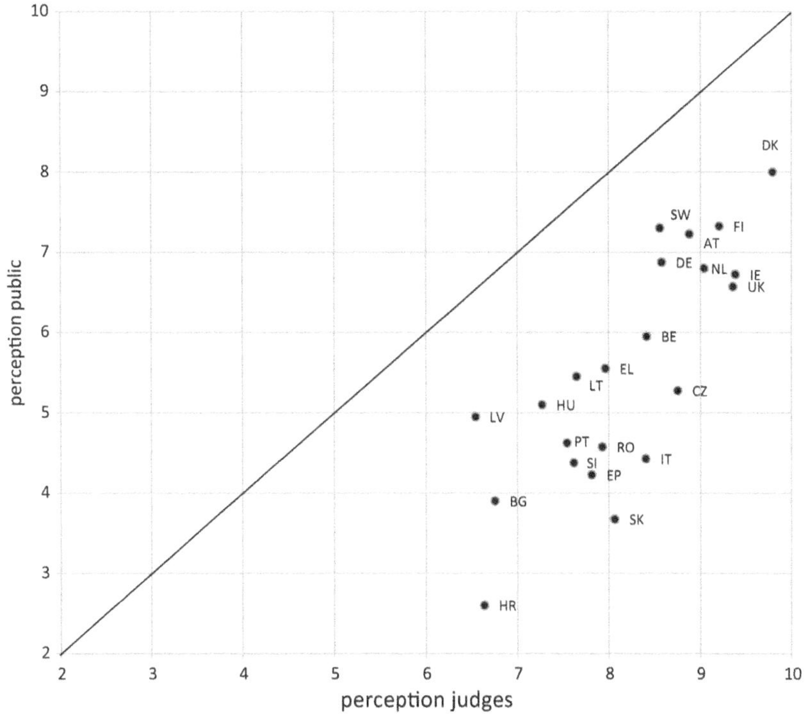

Fig. 3.1 Perceived judicial independence by public and judges, average per country (*Note* See list of country abbreviations at end of this chapter)

is independence "strong" or "weak"? While such doubts about independence may or may not be justified, the existence of negative perceptions are relevant in themselves, as was argued in Chapter 2.

It should be noted that the perceptions of the public reflect the appearance of independence, as the vast majority misses the knowledge and information to assess independence by examining the judicial decisions factually. Table 3.2 shows also that the perceptions of the public are highly correlated with those of the lawyers and with the perceptions of the judges. The differences among countries are not in doubt.

Level of education plays an important role in the assessment of independence: on average a high education leads to a more positive perception of independence, and low education to a less positive perception (EC 2019b). See Fig. 3.2. Across countries, the mean score falls from 5.7 for high education (finished education older than 20) to 5.1 for low education (left education younger than 15). The standard deviation for low

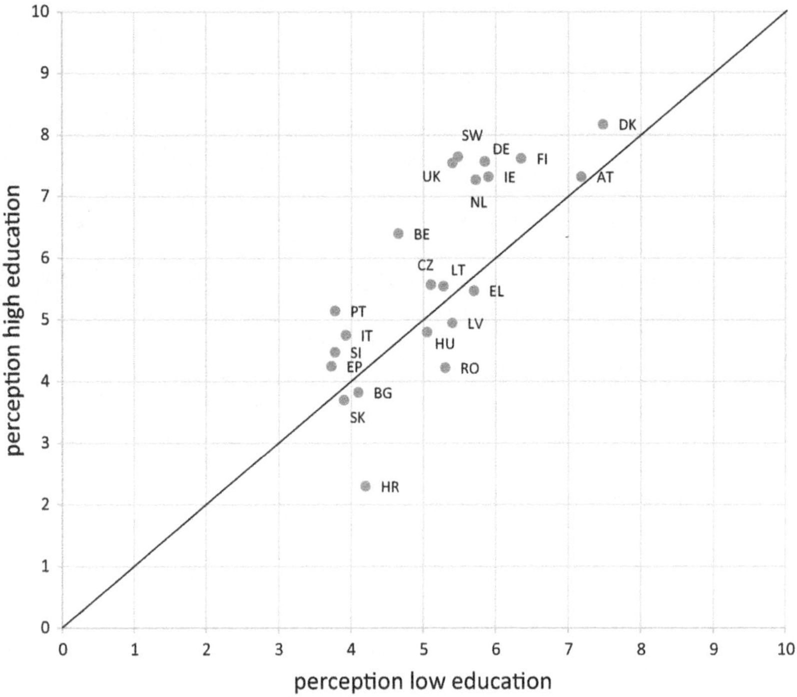

Fig. 3.2 Perceived independence by the general public, by level of education, average per country

education is smaller than that for high education (1.0 vs 1.6), suggesting that the latter persons are more discerning. For judiciaries with a very positive perception of independence by judges and lawyers the effect of different levels of education on the perceptions by the public is much larger than in judiciaries with a less positive perception. The difference is larger, the more positive the perception of independence by for instance lawyers.[8] If independence is compromised, citizens agree on that, irrespective of their level of education. If independence is strong, respondents

[8] Linear regression at country level: Ind Public High Edu − Ind Public Low Edu = 0.72** × Ind Lawyers − 4.04; $N = 17$; $R^2 = 0.65$. Thus, if Ind Lawyers is 10, the difference between high and low education is 3.2 points, while if Ind Lawyers is 5, the difference is −0.4 points.

with a high education recognize this better than respondents with a low education. For example, in Sweden citizens with high education score judicial independence at 7.6, while citizens with low education score at 5.5, which should be compared with the score by judges of 8.6 and by lawyers of 8.2. When perceptions of judges and lawyers are less positive, the difference is smaller. For instance in Lithuania, the scores are 5.6 and 5.3, to be compared with 7.7 and 5.9 of judges and lawyers.

In several countries where independence is in relatively low regard by judges and lawyers, the impact of education is reversed. In Romania citizens with high education give a score of 4.2 and with low education 5.3, and in Latvia 4.9 and 5.4. In Hungary, Slovakia and Greece the same effect can be observed, but to a lesser degree.[9] In all these countries citizens with low education believe that the judiciary is more independent than citizens with a high education. Not surprisingly, the perceptions about judicial independence of highly educated citizens are much more aligned with those of judges and lawyers than citizens with low education.[10] This may be due to differential exposure to accurate information and/or differing abilities to filter information accurately, but also to a better working of the judicial system for highly educated people. With regard to information persons with low education may be exposed to other media than persons with high education. The differential effect of sensationalist and serious media has been shown for the US (Johnston and Bartels 2010).

A consequence is that citizens with low education in countries that are quite distinct in the eyes of all other groups, may perceive the independence of their respective judiciaries similarly (see Fig. 3.2). This is the case for instance for Latvia and the UK, Romania and Sweden, and Greece and the Netherlands. This could explain why populist parties that draw support from among these groups often rally against judiciaries (see Chapter 7) and find internationally common ground. It is a concern that judiciaries lack connection with these segments of society.

Apart from education, the survey gives some other characteristics of the respondents (EC 2019b). The impact of these is smaller than of

[9] For Hungary the scores are respectively 4.8 and 5.1, for Slovakia 3.7 and 3.9 and for Greece 5.5 and 5.7.

[10] Across 17 countries correlation coefficients are 0.69** between perceptions by judges (all) and perceptions by citizens with high education, and 0.35 between perceptions of judges and perceptions by citizens with low education. The same correlation coefficients but with regard to the perceptions by lawyers are: 0.83** and 0.38.

education. As to age, young people are more positive about judicial independence than old people on average across countries. This holds for countries in Eastern Europe, but not for Western European countries. Geographical categories (rural villages, small/mid-size towns and large towns) do not show substantial differences. This is interesting, as populist support is often suggested to be higher outside the big cities.

The outcomes for citizens in Europe can be compared with the results for similar surveys in the US, where citizens (registered voters) are surveyed regularly about the functioning of the state courts. The sample is relatively small: 1,000. The questions do not address independence directly, but some questions are connected. In the survey that was held in November 2019, 54% of the respondents see the state courts as fair and impartial, 49% as unbiased in their case decisions, but 55% see state courts as political. This compares broadly with the Eurobarometer survey: 56% of the respondents perceive independence to be very good or fairly good for the EU28 (EC 2019b, Table Q1).

Can we get deeper into the opinions of the public? A comparison is possible with a one-off Eurobarometer survey commissioned by the European Commission about the rule of law: it focuses on the importance citizens attach to a range of aspects of the rule of law and the need for improvement of these aspects according to them (EU 2019c). Several aspects that the survey examines concern the existential notion of effective judicial protection by independent courts. In this context particularly relevant are the following aspects with the statements put to respondents in brackets: access to an independent court ("if individuals' rights are not respected, they can have them upheld by an independent court)", the independence of judges ("judges are independent and are not under the influence of politicians or economic interests"), respect for and application of court rulings ("public authorities and politicians respect and apply court rulings") and criticism on judges ("codes of conduct for politicians imposing limits on politicians criticizing courts and judges"). On all these four aspects around 50% of the respondents on average across countries see a definite need for improvement and another 30% answers "maybe somewhat". While the aspects just mentioned are very interesting, the answers are unfortunately not informative as they are extremely correlated (correlation coefficients 0.98 or 0.99 at country level). Also, the correlation is very high with the percentage of respondents that recognize a definite need to improve timeliness and costs of court procedures (0.85 and 0.86). The correlation with the above discussed perceptions of the public about independence is −0.74 (correlation between the independence score and the need for improvement of independence). The outcomes of both surveys are consistent in that respect. Apparently, the public has a rough idea of the independence of the courts, but does not distinguish between the aspects put to it. For the public, the aspects mentioned go hand in hand, and no specific aspects jump out. Consequently, it cannot be expected from the general public that it has an opinion about the deeper aspects of independence.

3.5 Independence as Perceived by Companies

A Eurobarometer survey is available about the perceptions of independence by companies (EC 2019a). This survey has the same design as the survey among the general public. The outcomes of the two surveys are highly correlated and the mean scores are very close to each other. For the 22 countries sample the mean is 5.6 with a range of 2.5 for Croatia to 8.6 for Denmark. Table 3.2 gives again the outcomes for the two subsets. For the two subsets the means are nearly the same for the public and for firms, and the correlation coefficients are very high.

The statistics hide underlying differences. There are very large "do not know" categories for some countries. Hungary (53%), Estonia (48%), Slovenia (30%), Lithuania (27%), Portugal (27%), Sweden (24%), and Poland (22%) have percentages above 20%. These percentages are much higher than those for citizens, for instance in Hungary (citizens 24%) and in Estonia (citizens 30%). This uncertainty could be caused by unfamiliarity of companies with the courts, but this is highly unlikely, given the prevalence of legal disputes in economic life that require court intervention (see the next section). If it may be assumed that firms are knowledgeable about the courts, the likely cause would be the political climate in the countries concerned, affecting the current and future independence of the courts in general or with respect to business litigation in particular. This uncertainty is likely to have negative effects on the behaviour of the companies for instance with regard to investment.

The size of companies seems to play a role (EC 2019a, p. 11). The survey is in this respect not more than indicative, as the number of participating large companies is small. The larger the company, the higher it's perception of judicial independence. On average across countries, the independence score of the smallest companies (1–9 employees) is 5.6, and that of the largest (more than 250 employees) 7.0.[11] Differences between countries are erratic probably due to the small number of observations.

3.6 Independence as Perceived by the Users of the Court

In this section the focus is on the parties in procedures. To elicit the opinions of these court users, two methods can be used. The first method makes use of a survey among the general population and filters out the respondents that have been to court. This method is used in the US, for instance, for the state courts (GBAO 2020). The Eurobarometer survey about independence among the public has not been designed with this purpose in mind, but distinguishes between citizens with and without experience with the courts by asking whether they have been involved in any dispute which went to court in the last two years (EC 2019b).[12] Only a small percentage of the public has that experience: across countries the mean is 6.2% with a range between 2% in Finland and Sweden and 8% in Portugal and Slovakia with Croatia as outlier with 12%. The absolute numbers per country are low: between 16 and 124 respondents with a median of 59. Still, it gives an impression. When comparing respondents with and without experience, results must be used with caution, as selection effects may occur. From a methodological point of view, the low number of respondents with recent experience can be resolved by oversampling (see e.g. World Bank 2018). The survey about companies contains the same question about experience as the survey among citizens.[13] The percentage of companies that have experience is 10.5% in the mean, with 3% in the UK and Sweden and 19% in Germany and Belgium with Croatia again as outlier with 28%. Absolute numbers of respondents with experience are low: between 6 and 75 with a median of 22.

The other approach to elicit the views of court users is a court user survey. In Europe only a small number of judiciaries are systematically conducting court user surveys, and of those only two include questions

[11] All across countries means of the perceptions by companies and by judges (all) and lawyers differ except for the comparison of lawyers and large firms.

[12] Dataset at https://data.europa.eu/euodp/en/data/dataset/S2199_474_ENG/resource/1fa91d65-09f1-4011-9ef9-c062cfe1752e.

[13] https://data.europa.eu/euodp/nl/data/dataset/S2196_475_ENG/resource/02e2b962-bfe0-4136-821a-aacc96089395.

about independence or related concepts such as impartiality (the Netherlands) and neutrality (Denmark). Such a survey is a major investment for courts, as the survey cannot be implemented by the Internet without selection effects. CEPEJ is promoting the use of court user surveys and has had success (CEPEJ 2018). These surveys, however, concern individual courts. To get an indication of the perceptions of court users at present, the Eurobarometer surveys have to be relied on, and the results can only be contrasted with the scant figures from court user surveys.

The question is whether experience has an impact on perceived independence. Effects of experience are likely, as the infrequent contacts of citizens, in particular, with the courts does not easily allow for the development of accurate expectations among the whole population. Also, personal experiences are likely to be varied due to the variety of court cases and their outcomes. Many factors play a role. In the first place, hands-on experience would lead to a better understanding of the workings of the courts and the behaviour of judges. This would lead to respondents being more opinionated than respondents without experience. Assuming largely uniform behaviour of judges within a judiciary, one would also expect more homogeneous replies: in the extreme, 100% would fall in one of the four categories of positive and negative answers that these surveys use, instead of a 'do not know' category. In the second place, a factor is the experience of going to court as such. For the US state courts it has been found that parties have lower confidence in the courts than people that do not have experience with the courts (Benesh 2006). Benesh argues that going to court is not a positive experience for parties. For them the stakes are high, but they have relinquished control over their situation. This is consistent with her finding that citizens that act as jurors and who have consequently low stakes and high control have more confidence. If such negative experience affects perceptions of independence also negatively, this would lead to parties rating the independence of the court lower than citizens with no experience. A similar finding was made by Wenzel et al. (2003) that suggests that the adversarial nature of the US legal system leaves scars.

In the third place, as discussed in Chapter 2, winning or losing one's case plays a role in the satisfaction of court users with the court, and this may have an impact on their perception of the independence of the court, whether or not justified. If winning or losing is dominant in the minds of the parties to such an extent that it determines their perceptions of independence, perceptions would be sharply divided. In the extreme, 50% of the parties is positive about independence and 50% negative, when court cases end in a winner and loser. This is, luckily, unrealistic. As discussed, procedural justice plays an important role, and reduces the relevance of winning and losing. Conversely, lack of procedural justice leads to more emphasis on winning and losing. Given varying degrees of procedural justice among judiciaries, this would result in differences in perceived independence among judiciaries.

Turning to the results of the surveys, Table 3.3 gives the summary statistics, while Fig. 3.3 presents the overall results in terms of the five answer categories of the survey, and the results for two judiciaries that display typical patterns. There are large differences between citizens and companies. What they have in common, is that experience leads to a reduction of respondents that have no opinion about judicial independence. With regard to citizens the category 'do not know' declines from 13 to 5%. See Fig. 3.3. For companies it declines from 16 to 5%.

As to the differences, the independence score awarded by citizens with experience is significantly lower than that of inexperienced citizens (5.0 vs 5.5 for 17 countries). See Table 3.3. This is the case for nearly all countries. Exceptions are few: Finland, Portugal, Slovakia and Romania. A lower score of more than 1 point is found for Germany, Ireland and the Netherlands.

The independence score of companies differs not significantly for firms with experience and without experience. The means, however, disguise big differences among judiciaries. There are countries with positive and with negative differences. Large positive differences due to experience are found for the UK, Czech Republic (more than 2 points), Austria, the Netherlands, Slovenia (between 1 and 2 points). Large negative differences are found for Latvia, Bulgaria, Hungary and Romania (more than 2 points). Thus, experience has a differential effect.

Table 3.3 shows also that perceptions of citizens with experience are less highly correlated with the perceptions of judges and lawyers than perceptions of citizens with no experience. This would be in line with the individualized experience of court users in which winning or losing plays a role. This effect is not observed for companies that seem to be more rational.

Perceptions tend to get more extreme. See Fig. 3.3. There is a tendency towards the extremes (very good; very bad) with experience in countries, where this is possible (in Denmark this is, for instance, not the case, as the upward effect of winning is truncated by the ceiling),

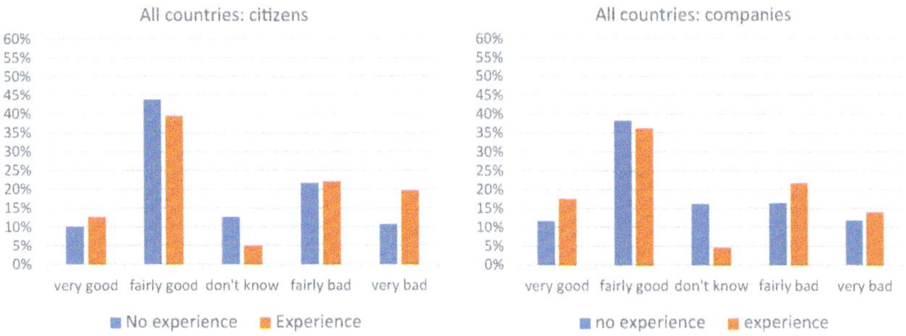

22 countries	public	companies
score no experience	5.5	5.6
score experience	5.1	5.7
% experience	6.1%	10.5%
# with experience	1,342	546
% extreme no exp	22%	24%
% extreme exp	33%	32%
% homogeneous no exp	36%	40%
% homogeneous exp	30%	48%

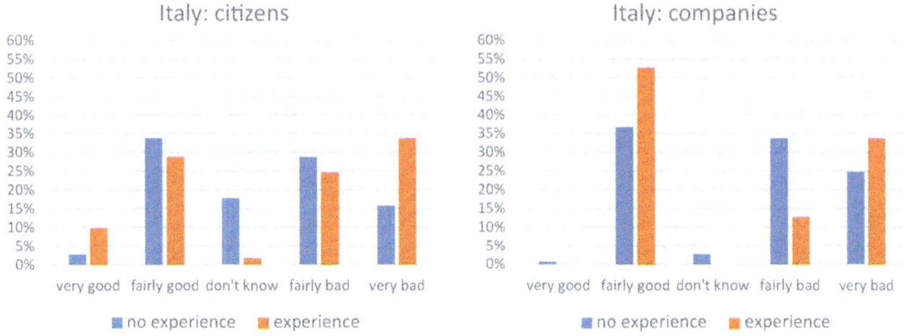

Italy	public	companies
score no experience	4.5	3.9
score experience	3.9	4.3
% experience	5.9%	5.7%
# with experience	59	22
% extreme no exp	19%	26%
% extreme exp	44%	34%
% homogeneous no exp	8%	21%
% homogeneous exp	20%	6%

Fig. 3.3 Score of judicial independence by the public and by companies, without and with experience with disputes in court, average for 22 countries and average scores for Italy and for Czechia (*Notes* [1] Experience: involvement in any dispute which went to court in the last two years; [2] Extreme: sum of answer categories 'very good' and 'very bad', for respondents with and without experience; [3] Homogeneous: absolute value of '(very) good' minus '(very) bad', for respondents with and without experience)

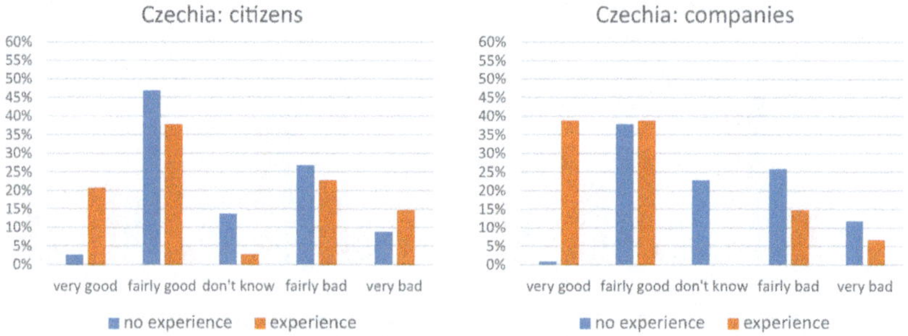

Czechia	public	companies
score no experience	5.2	4.7
score experience	5.7	7.2
% experience	7.6%	15.7%
# with experience	76	31
% extreme no exp	12%	13%
% extreme exp	36%	46%
% homogeneous no exp	14%	1%
% homogeneous exp	21%	56%

Fig. 3.3 (continued)

that can be attributed to the impact of winning and losing cases. "Very good" increases from 10 to 13% of citizens and from 12 to 18% of companies. "Very bad" increases from 11 to 20% for citizens and 12 to 14% of companies. In 14 out of 22 countries very good is higher for citizens with experience, and in 20 countries very bad is higher. Winning and losing seems to play a role for citizens in most countries. The impact on the perceptions of companies is more differentiated among countries.

The perceptions of citizens are less homogeneous for experienced than for inexperienced citizens, when measured as the percentages of very good and fairly good minus very bad and fairly bad. The absolute value of these differences across countries gives an indication whether respondents agree that the judiciary is independent or not independent. For citizens this percentage is lower for experience than for no experience (28 vs 35%). For companies, it is the other way round (48 vs 40%).

While the data allow only tentative conclusions, the main finding is that winning and losing has the most consistent effect, together with the reduction of uncertainty as such.

As mentioned before, the use of court user surveys that include questions concerning the independence or impartiality of judges is very limited in the countries examined here. This is telling about the mentality of the courts. Denmark and the Netherlands are conducting such surveys on a regular basis, the last one was in Denmark in 2013 (Oxford Research 2013) and in the Netherlands in 2017 (SAMR 2017). In Denmark the item of the survey that touches on independence is neutrality of the judge, and in the Netherlands impartiality of the judge. The survey method is totally different from the Eurobarometer, as the survey is administered in the courts. In Denmark 84% of the respondents replied that judges are neutral, 10% was indifferent or did not know and 6% answered that judges are not neutral. These outcomes compare with the results of the Eurobarometer for respondents with experience: 77%, 7% and 16% ($n = 36$), and without experience: 88%, 7% and 5% ($n = 966$).

For the Netherlands, in the court user survey 79% of the respondents answered that the judge was impartial, 16% was neutral or did not know and 5% responded that the judge was not impartial. The Eurobarometer collected much more critical responses: with experience 60%, 8%, and 32% ($n = 70$), and without experience 73%, 14% and 13% ($n = 927$). While differences are to be expected in view of the different questions and the different methodology, the outcomes are roughly consistent for Denmark but not for the Netherlands. More court user surveys are needed to enable a comparison of the two research methods. In addition court user surveys offer the possibility to differentiate the court users with respect to social and cultural background. Given the inequalities in society, this differentiation is particularly important (see e.g. Wenzel et al. 2003 on the US).

3.7 Explanations of the Differences of Perceptions

The main conclusion is that the perceptions among categories of actors, with the exception of the general public with low education, are highly correlated. At the same time perceptions differ substantially in level with judges generally being more positive about their independence than lawyers, and lawyers being more positive than the public in general, and in particular citizens with low education, as well as companies, and in particular small companies.

The impact of education is unexpected: the difference of the independence scores of citizens with high education and the scores of citizens with low education is positive and large in countries with a high level of independence according to judges and lawyers. When independence is perceived to be low, the differences disappear, and in some countries are even reversed. Citizens with low education are more positive about independence than citizens with high education.

As to the parties in law suits, the availability of data is an impediment. Also, the interaction of gaining more insight by personal experience in the independence of judges and the potential impact of winning and losing cases complicates the analysis. The data clearly indicate that people with experience are more opinionated about independence (much less 'do not know' answers are given), and also that opinions of persons with experience are more extreme than the opinions of those without experience, suggesting that winning and losing play a role. It was also found that the main score of independence for citizens with experience is lower than that for citizens without experience. This leads to an even larger distance to the perceptions of judges than the inexperienced public has. It must be noted that selection effects (for instance for citizens with respect to education and for companies firm size) may play a role, but this cannot be checked because of the data limitations.

What could explain the lack of alignment of judges and society? Two extreme explanations will be considered in the next chapters.

(1) Judges live in the often suggested ivory tower:

- Judges evaluate their independence too positively, consciously or unconsciously. They have a strong esprit de corps, are not open for criticism, and in denial about the workings of the legal system. They are focussed on their case work, and do not pay attention to the big picture.
- Lawyers are more critical than judges, but they are part of the judicial/legal system, benefit from it, and are therefore more positive than external observers would be.
- The perceptions of the court users and the general public may be biased, but, just because they are outsiders, their perceptions are more reliable and informative than those of judges and lawyers.

(2) The general public is not well informed about the courts, and biased negatively due to influence of media, social media and in some countries politics:

- Judges are accurate about judicial independence in general in their country, and their perceptions are reliable and informative.
- The perceptions of lawyers are affected by winning and, in particular, losing cases. Also, they are dependent on the judges, and lack control over the proceedings which as such is frustrating.
- Parties are affected by winning and losing, as was shown above, and more intensely so than lawyers. They also lack control to a larger degree than the lawyers, and they cannot recognize when justice is done.
- The general public is subject to (social) media influence. The media report selectively with an emphasis on sensational events and matters that have gone wrong. Negative events have a stronger and more lasting impact than positive events (Baumeister et al. 2001).
- Distrust of public institutions in general affects the perception of judicial independence by the public.

The next Chapter examines how citizens who take part in the judiciary as lay judges view the independence of the judiciary. In as far as lay judges are critical observers of the judicial system, their perceptions about judicial independence could be decisive in determining which of these two extreme explanations is most valid.

Abbreviations of Countries

AT	Austria
BE	Belgium
BU	Bulgaria
CZ	Czechia
DK	Denmark
EL	Greece
EE	Estonia
ES	Spain
FI	Finland
DE	Germany
HR	Croatia
IE	Ireland

IT	Italy
LV	Latvia
LT	Lithuania
HU	Hungary
NL	The Netherlands
PL	Poland
PT	Portugal
RO	Romania
SI	Slovenia
SK	Slovakia
SW	Sweden
UK	United Kingdom
EW	England and Wales
SC	Scotland

References

Baumeister, R.F., E. Bratslavsky, C. Finkenauer, and K.D. Vohs. 2001. Bad is stronger than good. *Review of General Psychology* 5 (4): 323–370.

Benesh, S.C. 2006. Understanding public confidence in American courts. *Journal of Politics* 68 (3): 697–707.

Buunk, B.P., and N.W. van Yperen. 1991. Referential comparisons, relational comparisons, and exchange orientation: their relation to marital satisfaction. *Personality and Social Psychology Bulletin* 17 (6): 709–717.

CEPEJ. 2018. European judicial systems: Efficiency and quality. CEPEJ Studies No 23.

ENCJ. 2018. Data ENCJ Survey on the independence of lay judges 2017–2018. encj.eu.

ENCJ. 2019. Independence and accountability of the judiciary: ENCJ Survey on the independence of judges 2019. encj.eu.

ENCJ and CCBE. 2019. Independence and accountability of the judiciary: ENCJ/CCBE Survey among lawyers on the independence of judges 2019. encj.eu.

European Commission. 2019a. Perceived independence of the national justice systems in the EU among companies. Flash Eurobarometer 475.

European Commission. 2019b. Perceived independence of the national justice systems in the EU among the general public. Flash Eurobarometer 474.

European Commission. 2019c. Rule of law. Special Eurobarometer 489.

GBAO. 2020. State of the State Courts, Survey analysis.

Giladi, E.E., and Y. Klar. 2002. When standards are wide of the mark: Nonselective superiority and inferiority biases in comparative judgments of objects and concepts. *Journal of Experimental Psychology* 131 (4): 538–551.

Johnston, C.D., and B.L. Bartels. 2010. Sensationalism and sobriety: Differential media exposure and attitudes toward American courts. *Public Opinion Quarterly* 74 (2): 260–285.

Landes, W.M. 1971. An economic analysis of the courts. *Journal of Law and Economics* 14 (1): 61–107.

Oxford Research. 2013. Brugerundersøgelse af Danmarks domstole 2013, udarbejdet for domstolsstyrelsen, bilag.

Posner, R.A. 1973. An economic approach to legal procedure and judicial adminis-tration. *The Journal of Legal Studies* 2 (2): 399–458.

SAMR. 2017. Klantwaardering Rechtspraak 2017; Landelijk rapport. https://www.rechtspraak.nl/SiteCollectionDocuments/landelijke-rapportage-KWO-2017.pdf#search=klantwaarderingsonderzoek%202017.

Svenson, O. 1981. Are we all less risky and more skilful than our fellow drivers? *Acta Psychologica* 47 (2): 143–148.

Wenzel, J.P., S. Bowler, and D.J. Lanoue. 2003. The sources of public confidence in state courts; experience and institutions. *American Political Research* 31 (2): 191–211.

World Bank. 2018. Montenegro—Experiences and perceptions of Judiciary's performance © World Bank.

CHAPTER 4

Perceptions of Lay Judges About Independence of the Judiciary

Abstract Lay judges are citizens with particular knowledge of and experience with the judiciary. The findings of a survey among the lay judges of ten judiciaries are examined in this chapter. It is found that the perceptions of lay judges of judicial independence, their own as well as that of the professional judges, are very similar to the perceptions of the professional judges. In addition, lay judges are most positive about their independence, when they participate in judicial panels together with professional judges and when they are taken seriously by the professional judges. For them, these conditions surpass sitting alone as a judge. Although selection effects may play a role, the results indicate that experience as a lay judge leads to a much higher appreciation of judicial independence than that of (highly educated) citizens in general. This in turn indicates that the views of the general public are too negative about judicial independence.

Keywords Lay judges · Judicial independence · Survey

This Chapter is joint work with Frank van Tulder Bart Diephuis of the Netherlands Council for the Judiciary. Preliminary results have been presented at the 2018 EGPA conference.

F. van Dijk, *Perceptions of the Independence of Judges in Europe*,
https://doi.org/10.1007/978-3-030-63143-7_4

4.1 Lay Judges and Judicial Independence

Lay judges are a potentially interesting group when one wants to know more about perceptions of the independence of the judiciary. First of all because they are judges in their own right, and therefore their own independence matters. In the second place, they have hands on experience in the judiciary, yet they have less vested interests in the judiciary than professional judges as their primary tasks lay outside the courts. They do not fall under the court hierarchy for their careers like judges (Schneider 2005). Also, they do not have an interest in the cases they adjudicate like the parties and their lawyers. Lay judges are in a position to be more objective about the judiciary than the professional judges as well as the parties and lawyers. Their perceptions of the independence of the whole system are particularly interesting when they fulfil their tasks together with professional judges. This they generally do.

The number of lay judges amounts to 250,000 in the EU, the UK and Norway.[1] The latter two countries are included because they participated in the survey discussed below. This number can be compared with 83,500 professional judges. It should be stressed that these figures concern the number of persons. In full time equivalents the number of lay judges is only a small but unknown fraction of this figure. The involvement of lay judges is very unevenly spread across countries. In 68% of the above judiciaries lay judges play a role. In the judiciaries that make use of lay judges, their numbers per 100,000 inhabitants range from 6 in Italy and 8 in Scotland through 37 in France and 112 in Germany to 174 in Denmark and a staggering 856 in Norway (CEPEJ 2018). According to CEPEJ lay judges are working in all areas of law, and in some countries this is actually the case (Denmark, Norway and, except family cases, Belgium). In other countries the participation is much more limited, such as in Scotland where only misdemeanour and minor criminal cases are handled by lay judges. Involvement in serious criminal cases occurs often: in 75% of the countries that have lay judges. Also, in specific areas of civil law such as labour law there is relatively often involvement of lay judges. Machura (2016) looks at the involvement of lay judges in civil proceedings. He concludes that a wide variety exists in the way lay judges are involved. See

[1] CEPEJ (2018, Table 3.6, p. 109). Data on lay judges for Greece were provided by the Supreme Judicial Council of Greece. Same sources for the other data on numbers of (lay) judges.

also Burgess et al. (2014) on lay person involvement in specialized labour courts that exist in some countries. Again, differences among countries are large.

The reach of the survey among lay judges of the ENCJ (see Table 3.1) is much smaller than that of the survey among professional judges, because, obviously, not all judiciaries deploy lay judges but also for administrative reasons such as difficulties in reaching lay judges. Ten Judiciaries participated in the survey. Scandinavia had a heavy presence in the survey, but all parts of Europe are represented. As background information, the survey shows how lay judges are deployed. Consistent with the discussion above, the dominant form of lay participation is lay judges taking part in mixed panels with professional judges adjudicating criminal cases, but a variety of settings occurs. See Table 4.1. Only in the UK and Italy lay judges sit without professional judges as dominant form. Some lay judges (approximately 6%) operate in several settings. On average across countries, 71% of all settings in which lay judges operate involves interaction with professional judges. In Italy and in the UK this percentage is

Table 4.1 Setting in which lay judges adjudicate cases: number of answers given by type of setting, as percentage of total answers

	Number of respondents	*Number of answers*	*Alone (%)*	*Together with other lay judges only (%)*	*Together with professional judges only (%)*	*Together with professional judges and lay judges (%)*
Belgium	805	918	12.6	2,0	4.9	80.5
Denmark	5,983	6,206	0.1	5.3	2.2	92.4
Greece	363	366	1.4	14.2	1.4	83.1
Italy	485	549	68.5	1.5	15.8	14.2
Norway	7,942	8,256	0.6	10.2	3.5	85.7
Poland	763	770	1.2	1.4	3.5	93.9
Slovenia	429	431	1.4	4.6	2.8	91.2
Sweden	2,611	2,733	0.3	2.7	2.6	94.4
UK: E&W	1,106	1,415	10.8	47.6	4.5	37.1
UK: Scotland	118	122	48.4	3.3	6.6	41.8
Total/Average across countries	20,605	21,766	14.5	9.3	4.8	71.4

Note Lay judges sometimes operate in several settings, and more than one answer is possible

much lower: 30% in Italy, 42% in England and Wales and 48% in Scotland. Still, in all countries many lay judges have direct experience with the way professional judges behave which is necessary for the purpose of evaluating the independence of the judiciary as a whole.

In the remainder of this Chapter the following topics will be discussed.

- The perceptions of lay judges of their own independence and of the independence of the professional judges. Perceptions are compared with those of the general public.
- Aspects of independence and the connection of these aspects with the overall perception of independence. The analysis focuses on the interaction of lay judges and professional judges in mixed panels. This interaction is informative about the attitudes of professional judges that in turn affect the independence of lay judges and their perceptions about the independence of professional judges.
- Comparison of the perceptions of lay judges with the perceptions of professional judges.

Table 4.2 provides the summary data. Like the professional judges, the lay judges in the judiciaries that took part in the survey are generally positive about their independence. The survey asked lay judges to rate their own independence as well as the independence of all the lay judges in their country.[2] The mean score on own independence over the 10 judiciaries was 9.0 on the 11-points scale from 0 to 10 (average across countries). 59% of the respondents gave their independence the maximum score of 10 and 21% a score of 9. Only 4% gave a score lower than 6. Independence of the lay judges in general is less personal as well as broader, as respondents may take aspects such as the selection of lay judges into account. The mean score was lower, 8.5 with 37% of the respondents awarding a score of 10 and 26% of 9.5% gave a score lower than 6. Examining the outcomes per country, the mean scores on own independence range from 8.7 in Italy to 9.4 in Scotland and on the independence of all lay judges from 7.5 in Italy to 9.3 in Scotland. The outcomes are very similar to the outcomes of the survey among professional judges for these countries.

[2] Literally: "On a scale of 0-10 (where 0 means "not independent at all" and 10 means "highest possible degree of independence") as a judge I am". Same, but: "the lay judges in my country are".

Table 4.2 Summary statistics of the perceptions of judicial independence of lay judges by lay judges (personally and all lay judges) and professional judges by lay judges, the perceptions of independence of professional judges (personal and general) by professional judges and the perceptions of independence by the general public, for 10 judiciaries

	Lay judges own	*Lay judges all*	*Lay judges on prof. judges*	*Professional judges own*	*Professional judges all*	*General public*	*General public edu+*
Mean	9.0	8.5	8.5	9.1	8.7	5.9	6.2
Min–Max	8.7–9.4	7.5–9.3	7.4–9.3	8.4–9.8	7.6–9.8	4.3–8.0	4.1–8.2
SD	0.3	0.6	0.7	0.4	0.8	1.3	1.6
Typical patterns							
Greece	8.9	8.1	7.4	8.9	8.0	5.6	5.5
Italy	8.7	7.5	7.8	9.3	8.4	4.4	4.8
Sweden	9.3	8.6	8.9	9.1	8.6	7.3	7.7
Correlations							
Lay judges own	1	0.89**	0.84**	0.69*	0.76*	0.90**	0.94**
Lay judges all		1	0.90**	0.63	0.83**	0.84**	0.90**
Lay judges on prof.			1	0.70*	0.86**	0.83**	0.90**
Prof. judges own				1	0.91**	0.79*	0.81**
Prof. judges all					1	0.82**	0.89**
General public						1	0.97**
General public edu+							1

Notes

1. BE, DK, EL, IT, NO, PL, SL, SW, UK EW, and UK SC
2. Correlation across countries. Significance: **0.01 and *0.05. See list of country abbreviations at the end of Chapter 3
3. Poland: scores for professional judges based on ENCJ survey 2017
4. $N = 10$ for all except general public; $N = 9$ for general public (no data for Norway)
5. Paired sample T-test of means on country level: the means do not differ (at 5% significance level) of: (1) *lay judges all* and *lay judges on professional judges*, (2) *Lay judges own* and *professional judges own*, *lay judges all* and *professional judges all*, and *lay judges on professional judges* and *professional judges all*

The lay judges were also asked to rate the independence of the professional judges in their country. The scores are nearly the same as those for the lay judges themselves: the mean score was 8.5 with 39% of the respondents awarding a score of 10 and 25% of 9.6% gave a score lower than 6. Examining the outcomes per country, the means range from 7.4 in Greece and Poland to 9.3 in Denmark. Across country correlations are high between all measures, except the personal independence scores of the professional judges, which we saw earlier as well. The first conclusion is that lay judges and professional judges have very similar views on actual independence. This extreme similarity is surprising.

The last two columns of Table 4.2 give the perceptions of the general public, overall and with a high level of education. While correlations are high, the large difference in level with the professional judges is repeated here for the lay judges. The second conclusion is, therefore, that lay judges are in the mean much more positive about the independence of the judiciary than the public in general, whether it concerns their personal independence, the independence of all lay judges or that of the professional judges. It might be assumed that lay judges are generally recruited from citizens with a higher education. The last column of Table 4.2 gives the outcomes for the part of the general public that has a high education. The impact of education is small for the countries that participated in the surveys. High education reduces the differences only a little, but increases the correlations, as would be expected.

These findings suggest that direct observation and participation in the adjudication of cases lead to higher appreciation of the work of judges. This presupposes that the opinions that the persons held before they became lay judges were similar to those of the (highly educated) general public. Alternative or complementary explanations cannot be ruled out. Cultural adaptation to the dominant professional judges, combined with lack of understanding what really goes on during trials, cannot be excluded as cause for positive perceptions. These findings show, however, similarity with the outcomes of research into the perceptions of citizens about the evaluation of evidence and the severity of sentences in criminal cases in the Netherlands: once citizens had to decide on sentences themselves with knowledge of the facts of the case, the initial view that actual sentences were too lenient disappeared, and the opinions of judges and citizens converged (Wagenaar 2008). In both situations the opinions of judges and citizens converge, while in the latter citizens and judges did not interact. Members of the public are apparently so unfamiliar with the judiciary that a large shift in opinions is possible, once the knowledge gap has been filled.

4.2 Interaction of Lay Judges and Professional Judges

The independence of lay judges is not entirely the same as that of professional judges. Lay judges have to relate with the professional judges, in particular when they participate in mixed teams, and they may heavily depend on them. An analysis of the independence of lay judges, therefore, needs to consider the interaction of lay and professional judges in mixed panels, as the dominant form of interaction.

An important issue in the literature about lay judges is whether lay judges have influence on decisions, when participating in mixed panels. Casper and Zeisel concluded in 1972 in an impressive, in depth study that "the traceable overall effect of the lay judges on the verdicts of the German criminal courts is indeed small" (Casper and Zeisel 1972, p. 189). The study finds that lay judges affect the verdict in only 1.4% of all cases. It notes that it is not known "whether lay judges feel encouraged or restrained in the performance of their duty by the professional judges that sit with them" (Casper and Zeisel 1972, p. 189). A similar view about the limited impact of lay judges in mixed teams is expressed for Sweden in Diesen (2001). The same conclusion is reached in Kutnjak Ivkovic (2003, 2007) about the impact of lay judges on the (quality of) decisions and their active participation in deliberations, but there other beneficial, social aspects are stressed, leading to a positive evaluation of mixed panels. Voigt (2009, p. 327) finds that "the effects of lay participation on the judicial system, a number of governance variables but also on economic performance indicators are rather modest." These findings raise the question whether the professional judges bolster the independence of lay judges or detract from their independence.

The survey among the lay judges allows an answer to this question from the perspective of the lay judges themselves. Using the survey data, an analysis of the factors that affect their perception of independence can be made. Table 4.3 presents the results of a regression analysis at the individual level. The dependent variable is the perceived independence of lay judges in general, and the independent variables are personal characteristics, perceived external and internal pressure and the interaction with professional judges. All variables prove to play a significant role. Here, it

Table 4.3 Determinants of perceived independence of lay judges, linear regression

	Perceived independence of lay judges		
Variable	*Variant 1*	*Variant 2*	*Variation*
Inappropriate pressure	0.46***	0.30***	0.21
Accepted bribes	0.21***	0.17***	0.10
Affected by a threat or an actual disciplinary or other action	0.24***	0.21***	0.09
Decisions affected by actions of the media	0.18***	0.12***	0.11
Decisions affected by actions using social media	0.14***	0.13***	0.12
Gender (0 = male, 1 = female)		−0.12***	0.06
Age (years)		0.01***	0.13
Number of cases		0.02	0.03
Resolved cases alone		0.04	0.01
Resolved cases together with professional judges		0.14***	0.04
Inappropriate influence of professionals in mixed panel		0.16***	0.15
Contribution taken seriously by professionals in mixed panel		0.29***	0.24
Had impact on decision in mixed panel		0.17***	0.16
Dummy per country is included	yes	yes	
R	0.17	0.22	
N	20,605	18,996	

Notes

1. Significance levels: *0.05, **0.01 and ***0.01
2. All variables, accept for individual characteristics, concern lay judges in general. For all variables higher, is better
3. Two variants: variant 1 includes only aspects of independence that are relevant for lay judges as well as professional judges; variant 2 is the full model
4. Last column gives an indication of the variation in perceived independence that can be attributed to the related variable in variant 2. In this measure the absolute effect (given in the former column) and the standard deviation of the variable in the survey are combined

is of particular interest that the survey not only includes questions about the setting in which lay judges adjudicate cases, but also contains questions about the quality of the interaction when they sit together with professional judges. While one would expect that lay judges feel most independent when they sit alone, the outcomes show otherwise. Lay judges feel most independent when they sit with professional judges and they are respected by these professional judges in the sense that (1) they experience no inappropriate influence of these judges, (2) their contributions are taken seriously by them and (3) they have an impact on decisions. These conditions are according to the survey generally met: on average across countries, respectively, 84, 88 and 75% of the respondents (strongly) agree with the statements about these three aspects. As a result, lay judges operating in mixed panels perceive on average the independence of lay judges in their country approximately 0.14 points higher than their colleagues sitting with only other lay judges and approx. 0.10 points higher than lay judges sitting alone. However, if lay judges score neutral or negative on all three of the items about the functioning of mixed panels, their perception of the independence of lay judges in the country is at least 0.75 points lower than that of their colleagues not sitting in mixed panels. Practically, this is not relevant, as only 1% of the responding lay judges in mixed panels are neutral or negative about all three aspects.

To conclude, most lay judges interact with professional judges in mixed teams, they experience this generally as positive, and they derive from this a positive perception about their independence. These outcomes are very different from the conclusions of the literature that we discussed. The difference may be caused by the countries that participated. For instance, Germany, the country studied by Casper and Zeisel (1972), did not participate in the survey. Apart from timeframe, the big difference is, however, the methodology, as here the survey among lay judges provides the data, while the study of Casper and Zeisel (1972) is based on a relatively small survey among professional judges. As the perceptions of lay judges themselves are the subject of this Chapter, the differences in outcome do not detract from the relevance of the survey in this context, but point to the need for more research in this rather neglected area.

4.3 What Do Lay Judges Think About Professional Judges?

As Table 4.2 shows, in the mean across countries there is no difference between the views of professional judges and lay judges about the independence of professional judges. At the national level, the means of judges and lay judges differ significantly when evaluated at the individual level.[3]

[3] T-test at individual level. Significance level: 0.1%, except Belgium 1% and Poland 5%.

Combining the data for England and Wales and Scotland, in 6 out of 9 countries lay judges are less positive about the independence of professional judges than the professional judges themselves. For instance, in Italy lay judges are more critical (7.8 vs 8.4) as well as in Greece (7.4 vs 8.0). The opposite occurs in three countries (Belgium, Slovenia and Sweden). For Slovenia the difference is substantial (7.6 vs 8.2). Even in countries where lay judges are more critical than professional judges about the independence of professional judges, their assessment is much closer to that of the professional judges than to that of the general public, educated or not. Also, in the view of the lay judges, the interaction between lay and professional judges is in general positive. It seems safe to conclude that there is no disconnect between judges and lay judges in the countries for which data are available. Although alternative explanations such as dominance of the professional judges who set the standards of behaviour that are uncritically followed by the lay judges cannot be ruled out, the gap between judges and citizens disappears, once citizens experience hands-on how judges work, and do the work themselves. If this is so, the general public is not well informed about the judiciary, and their perceptions of judicial independence are distorted. At the same time, lay judges are not able to bring the perception of the general public about independence in line with their own perceptions to the extent that the gap is closed between their perceptions and those of the general public.

References

Burgess, P., S. Corby, and P.L. Latreille. 2014. Lay judges and labor courts: A question of legitimacy. *Comparative Labor Law and Policy Journal* 35: 191–215.

Casper, G., and H. Zeisel. 1972. Lay judges in the German criminal courts. *The Journal of Legal Studies* 1 (1): 135–191.

CEPEJ. 2018. European judicial systems: Efficiency and quality. CEPEJ Studies No 23.

Diesen, C. 2001. The advantages and disadvantages of lay judges from a Swedish perspective. *Revue internationale de droit penal* 72: 355–363.

ENCJ. 2017. Independence, accountability and quality of the judiciary: Performance indicators 2017. ENCJ Report 2016–2017. www.encj.eu.

ENCJ. 2018. Data ENCJ Survey on the independence of lay judges 2017–2018. www.encj.eu.

Kutnjak Ivkovic, S. 2003. An inside view: Professional judges' and lay judges support for mixed tribunals. *Law & Policy* 25: 93–122.

Kutnjak Ivkovic, S. 2007. Exploring lay participation in legal decision-making: Lessons from mixed tribunals. *Cornell International Law Journal* 40: 429–453.

Machura, S. 2016. Civil justice: Lay judges in the EU countries. *Onati Socio-Legal Series* 6 (2): 235–254.

Schneider, M.R. 2005. Judicial career incentives and court performance: An empirical study of the German labour courts of appeal. *European Journal of Law and Economics* 20: 127–144.

Voigt, S. 2009. The effects of lay participation in courts; A cross country analysis. *European Journal of Political Economy* 25: 327–339.

Wagenaar, A. 2008. Strafrechtelijke oordelen van rechters en leken: bewijsbeslissingen, straffen en hun argumentatie. Research memoranda 2/4. Netherlands Council for the Judiciary.

CHAPTER 5

Respect for Judicial Independence

Abstract This Chapter examines whether judges feel that their independence is respected. Three categories of actors are distinguished: the court users, the political system and the internal decision makers of the judiciary. Judges feel in the mean most respected by the internal leadership, to a lesser extent by the court users and least by the political system. In some countries judges do not feel respected by the political system at all. In the opinion of the judges, respect by the different actors has different features. Perceived respect shown by litigants has to do with absence of bribery and other forms of corruption, and inappropriate pressure. Respect by government and parliament is about the implementation of judgments by government and the case load of the judiciary. Case load depends on the resources that politicians make available. Respect by court management concerns absence of pressure on judges to adjudicate cases timely, case load and promotion of judges based on merit. Caseload is a recurring determinant of perceived respect for independence. This suggests that independence is highly affected by resource allocation.

Keywords Respect for independence · Survey · Politicians · Court users · Leadership

F. van Dijk, *Perceptions of the Independence of Judges in Europe*,
https://doi.org/10.1007/978-3-030-63143-7_5

5.1 Respect for Independence by Categories of Actors

The survey among judges provides insight into the extent to which judges feel that their independence is respected by a range of actors.[1] Their perceptions may of course differ from the respect these actors themselves believe to have or express for the independence of the judiciary. Judges observe the behaviour of these actors in court and, for instance, at the macro level in budget allocations to the judiciary, and therefore can provide insight in the respect shown in behaviour instead of only in words. Obviously, judges may have distorted observations or incentives to distort their observations in a survey to influence outcomes. Also, opinions of actors may differ about what respect or due regard for judicial independence actually is. Still, the opinions of those at work in the courts are particularly relevant to understand what the judiciary needs to function independently. As discussed in Chapter 2, respect for judicial independence throws light on the legitimacy of the judiciary. This approach also allows differentiation and comparison between categories of actors. In the next Chapter the perspective of the general public is considered.

For the professional judges the actors that they deal with fall in three categories: (1) the court users: parties, their lawyers and, in criminal cases, prosecutors, (2) the political system: government, parliament and the (social) media, and (3) the leadership of the judiciary: the highest courts (Supreme court, Constitutional Court) and the governance institutions of the judiciary (court management including the president of the court, councils for the judiciary, associations of judges). These are very different categories: the behaviour of participants in judicial procedures is relevant for day to day court cases. Judges interact directly and intensively with them. While there is good reason to show deference to the judges in court given their position of power, this does not preclude participants to try to influence judges inappropriately, such as by bribery in any form, threats, attempts to get judges off cases and attempts to influence case allocation.

The political system that consists of parliament and government in conjunction with the traditional media and to a lesser extent the social

[1] Statement in survey (ENCJ 2019): "In the last two years, I believe that my independence as a judge has been respected by [actor]". Five answer categories offered as to (dis)agreement with the statement.

media operates at the systemic level of legislation and resource allocation. Government and, to a lesser extent, parliament are also often involved in some way in the appointment of members of the highest courts and the governance institutions like councils for the judiciary,[2] but they can also attempt to intervene in individual court cases. And government itself is involved in court procedures. In these cases it is particularly relevant whether government abides by the judgments, also when these judgments go against the interest of government. In addition, politicians can express opinions about the judiciary, and influence public opinion. These roles can be played in different ways: by honouring the division of the powers of the state, providing sufficient resources, showing restraint as to influence on appointments and, if involved, by supporting appointments on merit, implementing judicial decisions, not criticizing the judiciary pending court cases and unduly, not doubting the democratic legitimacy of the judiciary, and so on. Or politicians can pursue the opposite. In pure form examples of the first approach can be found in Scandinavia and of the second approach in Poland and Hungary (e.g. Kovács and Scheppele 2018).

In a democracy the media play a crucial role in informing the public and politics about what goes on in the courts and in court cases. They can do this in various ways. State controlled media in particular may exhibit political bias, and influence public opinion in the direction the government wants. Poland is again a case in point. While not owned or controlled by the state, media can be politically associated with political parties to similar effect. An extreme example was set in the United Kingdom where justices of the Supreme Court were depicted as enemies of the people, when the Supreme Court decided against the government in a Brexit related case.[3] On social media similar phenomena can be observed. Media differ in their approach. Johnston and Bartels (2010) distinguishes sensationalist and sober media. It finds that sensationalist media reduce the support for the American courts on specific issues but also in general.

[2] See EC (2020) and ENCJ (2020) for the institutional arrangements in EU countries.

[3] Front page of the *Daily Mail* on 4 November 2016 under the heading: "Enemies of the people, Fury over 'out of touch' judges who defied 17.4m Brexit voters and could trigger constitutional crisis", and which starts with: "MPS last night tore into an unelected panel of 'out of touch' judges for ruling that embittered Remain supporters in Parliament should be allowed to frustrate the overwhelming verdict of the British public."

The internal independence of judges is determined by the judicial hierarchy, explicit or implicit, within and between courts but also by court management, for instance relating to human resource decisions. While judges may be fully independent in their judgments, career considerations make them dependent on the authorities, such as the president of the court, that have the power to make these decisions (see Schneider 2005). Whether judges let their behaviour be guided by this dependence, is another matter. As mentioned before, the ENCJ survey shows that many judges feel that, in particular, promotion decisions are problematic from the perspective of judicial independence (ENCJ 2019, p. 34). In this Chapter respect for independence is discussed in a national context. The influence of EU institutions will be considered in the next Chapter.

Table 5.1 provides the key statistics. Results are expressed as scores on a scale of 0–10 as before, for ease of comparison, and are recalculated from five answer categories. The Table gives correlations within the three categories of actors. While correlations are moderate to high among most combinations across categories, the perceived respect for judicial independence by the actors in the first two categories are very highly correlated. The third group draws a much more heterogeneous response, where constitutional courts are much less integrated than, for instance, supreme courts in the judicial system. Not depicted in the Table, the perceived respect from supreme courts is highly correlated with that from parties and lawyers. Also not depicted, prosecutors are not only participants in trials but also close to the judiciary or part of a joint magistrature. This explains the perception of high respect from prosecutors for judicial independence. With regard to the actors in the political system, the across country means of government and parliament as well as the means of media and social media are indistinguishable. The means for the court users differ significantly, while the internal actors show varied outcomes (see note 2 of Table 5.1).

Most judges report that their independence is respected by parties, lawyers and prosecutors. The score of 7.4 for the parties corresponds with 75% of the judges agreeing with the statement that their independence is respected, 15% being uncertain and 10% disagreeing. In the eyes of the judges much less respect is shown by the other state powers and the media (the score of 6.1 for government corresponds with percentages of, respectively, 54%, 20% and 25%). Judges experience even less respect from the traditional media. There are not many countries in which the relations are better with the media than with politics. Only Denmark, the Netherlands

Table 5.1 Respect for independence as perceived by judges by categories of actors, for 24 countries of Europe

Actors	*Mean*	*Min–Max*	*SD*	*Selected correlations*				
				Parties	*Lawyers*	*Prosecution*		
Parties	7.4	6.0–9.5	0.9	1	0.90**	0.88**		
Lawyers	7.8	6.0–9.5	1.0		1	0.90**		
Prosecution	8.4	6.9–9.6	0.7			1		
				Parliament	*Government*	*Media*	*Social media*	
Parliament	6.2	3.6–8.9	1.4	1	0.96**	0.93**	0.77**	
Government	6.1	3.5–8.7	1.6		1	0.91**	0.74**	
Media	5.7	3.8–8.7	1.6			1	0.87**	
Social Media	5.6	3.9–7.9	1.1				1	
				Supreme court	*Constitutional court*	*Court management*	*Council for judiciary*	*Judges association*
Supreme Court	8.6	7.5–9.6	0.7	1	0.59*	0.71**	0.62**	0.84**
Constitutional Court	8.3	7.3–9.5	0.9		1	0.06	0.54	0.68**
Court management	8.2	6.5–9.6	0.7			1	0.54*	0.51**
Council for judiciary	7.8	6.0–9.4	1.0				1	0.57**
Judges Association	8.8	7.1–9.8	0.8					1

Notes

1. Country coverage: 24 countries as in Table 3.2, but England and Wales and Scotland instead of UK and including Norway

2. Paired sample *T*-test of means on country level: means are not significantly different of: (1) *parliament* and *government, media* and *social media*, (2) *supreme court* and *constitutional court, court management* and *constitutional court, council for judiciary* and *court management, association of judges* and *constitutional court*. All other combinations of means differ significantly (<0.05)

and Romania are exceptions. While the social media get the same mean score as the traditional media, judges are much more uncertain about their relationship with social media: 35% of the respondents is uncertain, compared to 22% for the traditional media. Given the diverse and fluid character of social media, this is understandable.

Internal independence is well respected with generally higher scores than the scores of the other two categories of actors. The lowest scores are reserved for Councils for the Judiciary (7.8 with the corresponding percentages 77%, 13% and 10%), but their mean score is still at a different (higher) level than that of government and parliament.

5.2 Content of Respect for Independence

Respect for independence has a distinct content for the three categories of actors. This can be checked by examining the factors that relate to the respect variables. The ENCJ survey among judges examines a wide range of constituent elements of independence, and these elements can be used. Linear regression is applied at the level of judiciaries. Table 5.2 summarizes the outcomes. Respect by citizens as perceived by judges is related to corruption (such as bribery) and inappropriate pressure that judges experience. Respect by government and parliament depends primarily on the resources made available for the judiciary as reflected in the case load of judges, and on the implementation of judgments that go against the interest of government. The latter factor plays a role for the prosecution as well. This reflects the concerns of the judiciary of not being taken seriously. A judge can be totally independent in her court room, but if her judgments are not implemented, her independence is fundamentally flawed. The respect for independence by the media connects to a statement in the survey about the impact of the media: "decisions or actions of individual judges have, during the last two years, been directly affected by the actual, or anticipated, actions of the media (i.e. press, television or radio)". There is a strong relationship between respect from the media and the replies to this statement. The differences between countries are large: in Portugal only 25% of judges feels respected by the media, and, consistently, 50% believes judgments and behaviour of judges is affected by the media. In contrast, in Ireland 71% feels respected and only 4% sees an impact on behaviour of judges. The exception is England and Wales: a very low 27% of judges feels their independence respected, but only 6% sees an impact. The second variable that affects respect of the media is disciplinary action to influence judicial decisions. Here, causality is not evident, except that disciplinary measures are newsworthy events and can get magnified in the press. Respect by court management is related to the pressure exerted by management on judges to decide cases in a timely fashion, case load and the promotion of judges. Councils for the judiciary are apparently also seen as responsible for case load. Supreme Courts are expected to take a leadership role. These courts are associated with the

Table 5.2 Determinants of respect for independence by selected actors as perceived by judges, linear regression

Actors	*Determinants*	*Stand. B*	*Sign.*	*Adjusted* R^2
Parties in procedures	Corruption	−0.535	0.001	0.59
	Inappropriate pressure	−0.405	0.011	
Lawyers	Corruption	−0.364	0.007	0.85
	Disciplinary action	−0.335	0.004	
	Media pressure	−0.382	0.003	
Prosecution	Implementation	0.617	0.000	0.64
	Inappropriate pressure	−0.344	0.020	
Government	Case load	−0.497	0.004	0.54
	Implementation	0.420	0.012	
Parliament	Case load	−0.467	0.006	0.53
	Implementation	0.443	0.009	
Media	Media pressure	−0.416	0.027	0.51
	Disciplinary action	−0.428	0.023	
Court management	Pressure on timeliness	−0.475	0.001	0.74
	Case load	−0.445	0.001	
	Promotion	−0.337	0.018	
Council for judiciary	Case load	−0.702	0.001	0.46
Supreme Court	Implementation	0.559	0.000	0.72
	Case load	−0.285	0.026	
	Inappropriate pressure	−0.300	0.021	

Dependent variable: perceived respect of independence by [actor], score
Independent variables: statements of survey, percentage (strongly) agree:
Corruption: In my country I believe that during the last two years individual judges have accepted bribes or have engaged in other forms of corruption as an inducement to decide case(s) in a specific way
Inappropriate pressure: During the last two years I have been under inappropriate pressure to take a decision in a case or part of a case in a specific way
Disciplinary action: During the last two years I have been affected by a threat of, or actual, disciplinary or other official action because of how I decided a case
Media pressure: I believe that in my country decisions or actions of individual judges have, during the last two years, been inappropriately affected by the actual, or anticipated, actions of the media (i.e. press, television or radio)
Case load: I believe that changes which occurred in my working conditions in relation to case load directly affected my independence
Implementation: In the last two years, I believe judgements that went against the interests of the government were usually implemented/enforced in my country
Pressure timeliness: During the last two years the management of my court has exerted inappropriate pressure on me to decide individual cases within a particular time
Promotion: I believe judges in my country have been promoted or appointed other than on the basis of ability and experience during the last two years

implementation of judgments and the case load of judges. Also, inappropriate pressure is significant, indicating that supreme courts not only play a beneficial role. All variables have the expected sign.

The results are generally intuitive. What is striking is the large role of case load in relation to respect for independence. Lack of resources apparently permeates the judicial system, and many actors are held responsible, although judges clearly understand where the bucket ends: with government and parliament. Also, the small role of appointment and promotion issues is remarkable. Only, a relation exists between promotion of judges and respect for independence by court management. It seems that judges focus on their day to day work in court, and less on system wide issues.

5.3 Differences Among Countries

As follows from the descriptive statistics of Table 5.1, large differences exist among countries, in particular with regard to respect of independence by politics and media. Figure 5.1 maps the country scores of perceived respect for independence by parties to judicial proceedings and parliament, as representative of, respectively, court users and the political system. The perceived respect by these two actors is positively correlated (Table 5.1), and the difference between the two actors decreases with the increase of one of the scores.

The low scores of Bulgaria, Latvia and Romania reflect that only around 20% of the judges feel that their independence is respected by parliament and government. For respect from the media outcomes are similar. On the other hand, 80–90% of judges feels respected in the Scandinavian countries. England and Wales score surprisingly low with 36% and 37% of the judges feeling respected, respectively, by parliament and government, 27% by the traditional media and 17% by the social media. As to the parties and lawyers, a much higher respect score for both of them than for politics and media does not imply that the legitimacy of the judiciary in the eyes of the users of the courts is at an adequate level. For instance, in Bulgaria and Latvia in the order of 50% of the judges feels respected by parties and lawyers. Is this sufficient for a judiciary to function effectively? It must be noted that the percentage of judges that feels not respected by the parties is relatively low (17% in Bulgaria and 15% in Latvia). Many judges (in Bulgaria 30% and Latvia 38%) do not know whether parties respect their independence. It does not seem that these judiciaries—and other judiciaries as well—are positively legitimized by the

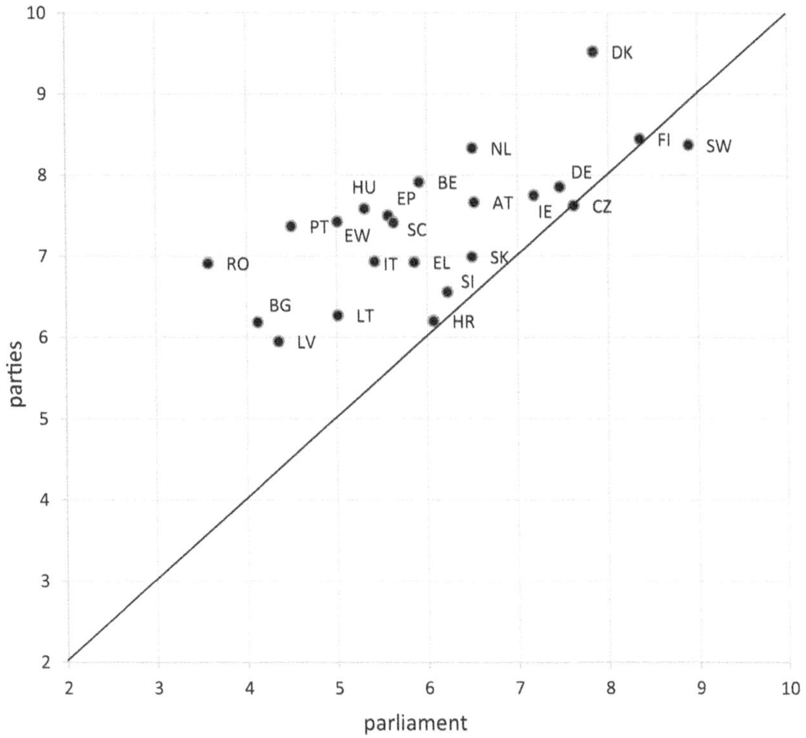

Fig. 5.1 Respect of independence of the judiciary by parties to judicial proceedings and parliament, average per country (*Notes* Scores between 0 and 10; See list of country abbreviations at the end of Chapter 3)

population to fulfil their mission, and thus they have a double problem: in the political arena and in the court room.

As to the internal actors, judges generally feel respected by the highest judges and by court management. Most variety, apart from several constitutional courts having specific issues, is shown by councils for the judiciary, reflecting different mandates, institutional arrangements but foremost actual behaviour of councils: percentages vary from around 55% of judges feeling respected by councils in Romania, Portugal and Spain up to 90% in Slovakia, Denmark and the UK.[4] The developments in Poland have made abundantly clear that within a few years a council can play very different roles, varying from protecting the independence of the judiciary to endangering independence by extending the influence of the government within the judiciary. Court management is generally seen as being respectful for independence. The lowest scores are found for Portugal (59% of the judges feels their independence respected) and Latvia (69%). Only Portugal combines relatively low scores for court management and council for the judiciary, pointing to serious internal governance issues.

To summarize, the categorization in court users, the political system and internal actors (highest courts and governance institutions) makes it possible to analyse the main issues the courts face. The issues about independence are largest between judiciary and politics, and play out in resource allocation and implementation of judgments. Respect for independence is much higher among the court users. This does not imply, however, that the respect by the court users is at a high level in all countries. The legitimacy of the judiciary is in several countries an issue. It is, however, difficult to draw a line between judiciaries with and without sufficient legitimacy. In Chapter 7 this is further discussed. The leadership of the judiciary generally respects judicial independence.

References

ENCJ. 2019. Independence and accountability of the judiciary: ENCJ Survey on the independence of judges 2019. encj.eu.

ENCJ. 2020. Independence, accountability and quality of the judiciary: Measuring for improvement, ENCJ Report 2019–2020. www.encj.eu.

European Commission 2020. 2020 EU Justice Scoreboard.

Johnston, C.D., and B.L. Bartels. 2010. Sensationalism and sobriety; Differential media exposure and attitudes toward American courts. *Public Opinion Quarterly* 74 (2): 260–285.

Kovács, K., and K. Scheppele. 2018. The fragility of an independent judiciary: Lessons from Hungary and Poland—And the European Union. *Communist and Post-Communist Studies* 51: 189–200.

Schneider, M.R. 2005. Judicial career incentives and court performance: An empirical study of the German labour courts of appeal. *European Journal of Law and Economics* 20: 127–144.

[4] In England and Wales and Scotland, councils are non-executive bodies, in contrast to the continental councils.

CHAPTER 6

Independence and Trust

Abstract The Chapter examines the trust of the general public in the judiciary at the national and EU-level. The starting point is that the correlation between the independence of the judiciary as perceived by the general public and the trust in the judiciary by the same public is very strong: trust in the judiciary equals trust in the independence of the judiciary. Trust in the judiciary is generally higher than that in parliament and government. However, the trust in the judiciary is generally at the same level as that in the public administration. It is likely that the general public associates the public administration with desirable, fair and impartial implementation of public policies, and not so much with (divisive) policy formation. Thus, it is too simple to conclude that the judiciary performs better than the other powers of the state. High trust in the judiciary is fostered by the nature of the tasks. At the EU-level the differentiation of trust between the three branches of government is much smaller than at the national level. Trust in the European Court of Justice (the supreme court of the European Union) is higher than in the national judiciary at low levels of trust at the national level, and smaller at high levels of trust. Still, trust in the ECJ is higher in countries with a highly trusted judiciary than in countries with a less trusted judiciary.

Keywords Trust · Judiciary · Public institutions · European Union · European Court of Justice

F. van Dijk, *Perceptions of the Independence of Judges in Europe*,
https://doi.org/10.1007/978-3-030-63143-7_6

6.1 Connection Between Independence and Trust

Several international surveys exist about trust in institutions. The European Commission has been organizing public opinion surveys for many years. These surveys among the general public in the member states of the EU record trust in national institutions including the national "justice/legal system" and in EU institutions, including the European Court of Justice (formally, the Court of Justice which as supreme court constitutes together with the General Court the Court of Justice of the European Union). While these surveys have as disadvantages that the definition of the justice/legal system is imprecise, and that the answer categories do not allow much distinctiveness (only three categories), the breadth of the surveys makes them particularly relevant for this study. The judiciary is the most important part of this potentially broader concept, and, for ease of exposition, the 'justice/legal system' will be denoted by the 'judiciary' in the sequel. As discussed in Chapter 2, trust in the judiciary and perceptions of judicial independence by citizens are connected. Applying the Eurobarometer survey on judicial independence and the public opinion survey on trust in the judiciary, the correlation between independence as perceived by citizens and trust by citizens, is 0.95. See Table 6.1. The correlation between perceived independence by companies, which is more based on direct experience with the courts and rational considerations than the perceptions of citizens, and trust of citizens is also high. As discussed before, it is likely that a positive perception of independence fosters trust in the judiciary, but reverse causality cannot be ruled out: people may trust the judiciary, and therefore believe in and respect its independence. For citizens independence of and trust in the judiciary are connected to such an extent that both are not distinguishable: trust in the judiciary seems to be foremost trust in the independence of the judiciary. Given this connection, it is also of interest for the study of judicial independence to compare the trust in the judiciary with the trust in the other branches of the state. It will be shown that independence and impartiality play a role in the trust of citizens in the other state powers as well. Two levels of institutions will be examined, national and European Union.

Table 6.1 Pearson correlations of the perception of independence of and trust in the judiciary for 25 countries of Europe

	% of public that tends to trust	*% of public that rates independence as (very) good*	*Score of public on independence*	*% of companies that rates independence as (very) good*	*Score companies on independence*
% public that trusts	1	0.93**	0.95**	0.77**	0.85**
% (very) good, public on independence		1	0.99**	0..87**	0.93**
Score public on independence			1	0.85**	0.94**
% (very) good, companies on independence				1	0.95**
Score companies on independence					1

Note 25 countries: 22 countries as in Table 3.2 and Estonia, France and Poland
Source perceived independence by the general public and by companies, as before (Table 3.1)
Trust in legal/justice system by the general public: European Commission, Eurobarometer Interactive, Public opinion survey June 2019, data 06/2019. Three answer categories: tends to trust, tends not to trust and don't know. https://ec.europa.eu/commfrontoffice/publicopinion/index.cfm/Chart/index

6.2 Trust in National Institutions

Trust in the three powers of the state differs widely among the countries of the EU (see also Sapignoli 2018). According to the public opinion surveys of the EC, trust varies from Croatia, where an extremely low percentage of 17% of the respondents tends to trust the judiciary and an even lower 13% both of the other state powers, to Finland, where 86% tends to trust the judiciary, 64% parliament and 56% the government. Not surprisingly, the outcomes for the three powers of the state are correlated. Still, substantial differences exist. Table 6.2 provides the summary data. The surveys show that in the mean trust in the national judiciary is higher than in the national parliament and the national government. According to the opinion surveys of the EC, higher trust in the judiciary than in parliament and government is found in most countries: in 16 out of the 25 EU-members that are included in this analysis. This is the case in all vested democracies, excluding Portugal and including Greece, while in Central Europe the Czech republic, Romania and Estonia exhibit this pattern. The gap between trust in the judiciary and that in the other powers of the state is often large in these countries, with the UK having an extreme gap of 38%-point. The decision making process on Brexit has reduced trust in both government and parliament, and only the judiciary is left standing. In most (12) of these 16 countries parliament and government are trusted to the same extent. However, in Scandinavia trust in Parliament is higher than in government. The reverse is seen only in the Czech republic. Apparently, in vested democracies trust is not evenly distributed among the state powers. This pattern is found in national surveys as well. For example for the Netherlands where each quarter trust in a range of institutions is measured (Dekker and Den Ridder 2020), and in Germany (Vaterrodt et al. 2018).

In contrast to the main pattern, in many countries of Central Europe and also in Portugal, in total 8 countries, the trust in the judiciary is equal to the trust in both other state powers (4 countries) or equal to the trust in one of them and higher than that in the other (four countries). A situation where trust in the judiciary falls below trust in the other state powers is only and only weakly found in Slovenia where 26% tends to trust the judiciary, 31% Parliament and 35% government. Based on older data, Grönlund and Setälä (2012) finds similarly that trust in the legal system is larger than in parliament, except for Spain and Slovenia, based on the European Social Survey. Considering the two groups of countries

Table 6.2 Summary statistics of trust of the general public in the state powers and the press for 25 countries of Europe (percentage of respondents that tend to trust)

	Judiciary (Justice/legal system)	*Parliament*	*Government*	*Press*
Mean	52%	36%	38%	49%
Min–Max	17–86%	13–71%	13–63%	27–76%
SD	19.3	17.2	13.7	13.2
Correlation				
Justice/legal system	1	0.85**	0.78**	0.66**
Parliament		1	0.89**	0.82**
Government			1	0.80**
Press				1
Order of trust	**J > P = G**	**J > P > G**	**J > G > P**	**J > G and J > P**
Number of countries	12 (AT, BE, EE, FR, DE, EL, IE, IT, NL, RO, ES, UK)	3 (DK, FI, SW)	1 (CZ)	16
Order of trust	**J = P = G**		**J = G > P**	**J = G and J ≥ P or J = P and J ≥ G**
Number of countries	4 (HR, HU, PT, SK)		4 (BG, LT, LV, PL)	8
Order of trust	**G = P > J**			**G > J and P > J**
	1 (SI)			1

Notes

1. 25 countries: AT, BE, BG, CZ, DE, DK, EE, EL, ES, IE, IT, FI, FR, HR, HU, LA, LT, NL, PL, PT, RO, SK, SL, SW, UK. See list of country abbreviations at the end of Chapter 3

2. Order of trust: J = Judiciary, P = Parliament and G = Government. Unequal if difference >5%-point (A–B<5 and B–C<5, then A=B=C, even if A–C>5)

3. **Correlation is significant at 0.01 level (2-tailed)

4. Paired sample *T*-test of means on country level: all means significantly different (<0.01) except *P and G* and *J and PR*

5. It should be noted that trust in the judiciary by citizens is related to perceived independence but it is also related to trust in the other state powers, as a simple regression analysis clarifies (For example: Trust in judiciary = 9.986** × Independence perceived by public + 0.331** × Trust in Parliament −15,733; adjusted $R^2 = 0.929$)

Source European Commission, Public Opinion, Eurobarometer Interactive. Trust in national institutions, data 06/2019, except Press 11/2018

together, it is quite obvious that the pattern of relatively high trust in the judiciary generally goes together with a relatively high level of trust in the other two institutions.

As noted before, in a democracy the press plays a vital role in reporting about the functioning of the branches of government which is not directly observable by the general public, but the media can also be under the influence of the government or parliament, directly or indirectly. Media under the influence of the judiciary have not been observed yet. On average 50% of the respondents tend to trust the judiciary. The same percentage is found for the press. The cross country variation of trust in the judiciary is somewhat larger than of trust in the press. Higher trust in the judiciary than in the press or equal trust is predominantly found in established democracies with Belgium, Italy and Portugal as exceptions. This is neither good nor bad, except when differences are extreme. Extreme more trust in the judiciary than in the press is found for the UK (difference of 29%-point), Ireland (17%), Denmark (22%) and Greece (26%). The reverse is found for Croatia (24%), Slovakia (18%) and Portugal (17%). These outcomes lead to interesting questions about the impact of reporting in the press on trust. It could well be that negative reporting ("enemies of the people") reduces the trust in the judiciary, but even more the trust in the press itself.

To check whether this pattern is specific for Europe, a comparison can be made with the United States where confidence of the general public in public institutions is measured as well. In 2019 the confidence in the judiciary stood at 69% for the US Supreme Court, 65% for the State Court system and 65% for the Federal court system (percentage of the respondents that answer that they have a great deal or some confidence; GBAO 2020). These levels of trust are higher than the European mean, and are comparable with the figure for Germany. Only in Scandinavia and the Netherlands trust in het judiciary is higher than the mean for the US. The comparison at the state level is most relevant here. Confidence in the State Courts (65%) is higher than in the State Legislature (58%) and Governor (59%). The differences are, however, smaller than in the EU. Thus, the same phenomenon is observed in the US, but in less extreme form than in the EU. It should be noted that in the US while the confidence in the judiciary increased since the start of the current surveys eight years ago until 2018, it sharply declined in 2019 (from 76 to 65%). The same happened to the other branches of government, but the decline hit the courts harder (Governor from 60 to 59% and State legislature from 65 to 58%).

Switching to the development over time over a longer period, since 2004, the first year when most current EU members participated in the survey, trust in the judiciary has increased on average with 20%. In contrast, trust in parliament declined with 6%, and in government it increased a little with 3%. Trust in the press increased over the whole period with 9%. Developments within the EU have been uneven. Departing from the average are in particular, negatively, Greece (judiciary: −13% decline, parliament: −36%, Government: −31%), Croatia (−7%, −12%, −13%), Spain (−2%, −24%, −26%), Romania (+13%, −10%, −19%), UK (+7%, −18%, −13%) and France (+13%, −11%, −2%), and positively: the Netherlands (+22%, +15%, +25%), Poland (+21%, +24%, +25%) and Sweden (+19%, +15%, +17%). These patterns are largely unsurprising, as they reflect the impact of the banking and sovereign debt crises that worked out differently across countries, and specific events such as Brexit. The results for Poland are intriguing, as they do not presage the current backsliding. Poland was one of the frontrunners in the accession to the EU and thereby in reforming its government/governance structure (Coman 2014).

These outcomes could easily lead to the conclusion that of the three branches of the state the judiciary is trusted the most. However, matters are more complicated. The public opinion surveys of the Eurobarometer also ask the public whether they tend to trust the public administration and the regional and local authorities in their country. Also trust in the police is regularly surveyed. See Table 6.3.

Average percentages of those who tend to trust institutions across countries are much the same for the judiciary, public administration and regional and local public authorities. In only seven countries the trust in the legal system is substantially higher than in both other public sector institutions. This group is dominated by North Western European countries. In all other countries trust is equal and more often lower than in the other institutions. The trust in the police (70% on average) is much higher than in the judiciary.[1] Only in Austria police and judiciary rank the same.

The conclusion is that the trust in the judiciary differs from trust in government and parliament but not from the trust in, what is called, the public administration and regional and local public authorities. It

[1] In the US confidence in the local police is expressed by 77% of the respondents in 2019, down from 89% in 2018. The difference in 2019 between state judiciary and police is smaller than in the EU (12 vs 18%-point).

Table 6.3 Summary statistics of trust of the general public in the public sector for 25 countries of Europe (percentage of respondents that tend to trust)

	Judiciary (Justice/legal system)	*Public administration*	*Regional and local public authorities*	*Police*
Mean	52%	51%	54%	70%
Min–Max	17–86%	24–75%	21–77%	45–93%
SD	19.3	15.5	15.3	14.2
Correlation				
Justice/legal system	1	0.85**	0.78**	0.85**
Public administration		1	0.96**	0.78**
Regional and local			1	0.72**
Police				1
Order of trust				
		J > PA: 8 (DE, FI, SW, NL, UK, EL, IT, RO)	**J > RL**: 7 (DE, FI, SW, NL, UK, IT, EL)	**J > POL**: 0
		J = PA: 7 (AT, DE, HU, EE, IE, LV, PT, ES)	**J = RL**: 7 (AT, HR, EE, IE, PT, RO, ES)	**J = POL**: 1 (AU)
		J < PA: 7 (BE, BU, HR, CZ, FR, LT, PL, SI, SK)	**J < RL**: 11 (BE, BU, CZ, FR, DE, LT, LV, PL, SI, SK)	**J < POL**: 24

Notes
1. **Correlation is significant at 0.01 level (2-tailed)
2. Order of trust: at least 5%-point difference
3. Paired sample *T*-test of means on country level: all means significantly different (<0.01), except *J and PA* and *J and RL*

Source European Commission, Public Opinion, Eurobarometer Interactive. Trust in national institutions, data 06/2019

is not self-evident how the respondents interpret "the government" and "the public administration". It seems likely that public administration is primarily seen as the implementer of public policies and the provider of public services. This reflects the classic distinction between policy development and policy implementation: the first is political, and the second should ideally be a political and impartial, being subject to judicial review. This separation from politics is made explicit for autonomous agencies and in particular for regulators that, largely stemming from EU-law, are fully independent from national political institutions, and whose independence is protected by the judiciary. Grönlund and Setälä (2012) make a distinction between representative institutions and institutions primarily responsible for implementing laws (in particular the judiciary), and argue that representative institutions require a certain level of distrust (see also Warren 1999).

If correct, the public administration is less political than the government, and has the potential to be more trustworthy for a broader spectrum of the population than the political institutions of government and parliament. Although less clear-cut, the same reasoning could apply to regional and local public authorities that provide local services. Given the strong connection between independence and trust with regard to the judiciary, it is conceivable that related concepts such as fairness and impartiality play a role in the minds of the respondents with respect to the other institutions. Of course, the independence of the judiciary is fundamental and guaranteed by formal safeguards, while the position of the public administration is ambivalent (Papadopoulos 2013). Still, the same values as to the application of rules may be shared: whatever the rules, people need to be treated equally. However, the reasoning can also work the other way around. The fact that the extent to which the judiciary is trusted does not differ much from the trust in the public administration, can also be caused by the judiciary not being as independent as it should be. A further consideration is that in a national context the judiciary may be part of a legal/judicial system that is not supported by all political parties, and, consequently, it is drawn into the political field.

To summarize, the nature of the mission of the judiciary, including the impartial interpretation of the law and protection of rights, can be expected to (but need not always) foster trust more easily than the political system can or even should. A normative conclusion that the judiciary functions "better" than political institutions is not warranted. The judiciary is more akin to public administration than to political institutions, and a comparison with the public administration is more informative.

6.2.1 *Trust, Knowledge and Politicization*

Citizens can and do distinguish the judiciary from political institutions (the government, the parliament), but does the general public see a difference between the judiciary and other public institutions? Are the institutions the same in terms of trust, as suggested above, or are citizens not aware of the differences? The rule of law survey of the EC that is discussed in Chapter 3 shows that knowledge about the judiciary does not go deep. At best, citizens have a general understanding of what the judiciary is about. As a result, people who do not have direct or indirect experience with the courts, fall back on their institutional trust in (the non-political part of) the public sector in general or even their dispositional trust (see Chapter 2). This lack of specific understanding about the judiciary could also (partly) explain why citizens who are lay judges have a very different, much more positive perception of judicial independence than citizens in general (Chapter 4).

The awareness of the public of the specific role and position of the judiciary is likely to be time and location dependent. In stable times citizens may be only superficially aware of the judiciary and its independence. It is, however, difficult to imagine that in Poland the struggle between judiciary and government has gone unnoticed to the general public. In Poland trust in the judiciary is roughly at the same level as trust in government and parliament, and much lower than in the public administration and the regional and local public authorities (37% versus 47% and 56% in June 2019). The politicization of the position of the judiciary in Poland shows in these figures. If we extend the reasoning that the position of the judiciary is likely to be politicized if trust in the judiciary falls short of the trust in the public administration and the regional and local public authorities, more countries are in this situation. For instance, Bulgaria, Slovakia, Slovenia and Lithuania, but also Belgium display this pattern to the same extent as Poland.

6.3 Trust in Multi-level Governance

The combination of the surveys about national institutions and EU institutions makes it possible to examine multi-level governance by comparing trust in the supranational institutions with trust in the institutions at the national level (see Arnold et al. 2012). In addition, the differences between the trust in the same European institutions, in particular the

European Court of Justice, by the citizens of the different member states can be examined, and related to trust at the national level. Table 6.4 shows that on average across countries the differences in trust between the state powers at the EU level are much smaller than at the national level. The European Court of Justice and the European Commission are actually indistinguishable trustwise, while the European Parliament stands apart from the European Court of Justice. As above, this raises the question whether respondents can differentiate between the EU institutions in the way they do nationally. According to another component of the public opinion surveys of the EC,[2] most people are aware of the existence of the European Parliament (93%), the European Commission (85%) and the European Court of Justice (71%), while people are much less aware of other EU institutions such as the European Ombudsman (41%) and the Economic and Social Committee (40%). The European Central Bank is well known as well (82%). Being aware is one thing, being able to differentiate between the performance of the institutions is another, but also the more technocratic nature of the EC than the political institutions at the national level may have an impact. If the EC is seen more as a public administration than national governments are, trust in the EC would be higher than in national governments for this reason alone. Table 6.4 shows also that the spread of outcomes for the national institutions among countries is much larger than for the corresponding EU institutions. This is not surprising as the same EU institutions are evaluated by the respondents, but of course in different ways across countries, while the national institutions differ as such.

On average across countries the trust in the justice system at the EU level is the same as at the national level, while the trust in the other state powers is much lower nationally than at the EU level. This fits in with the notion that the national courts and the ECJ and by extension the ECHR form one judicial system with the rule of law at its core ("national judges are European judges").[3] Its level of integration is higher than that of the national governments and the EC as well as the national parliaments and the EP.

[2] EC (2019). Public opinion, Awareness of the EU institutions. Data November 2019. https://ec.europa.eu/commfrontoffice/publicopinion/index.cfm/Chart/index.

[3] E.g. Frans Timmermans, Vice President of the EC, on Twitter 21 February 2019.

Table 6.4 Summary statistics of trust of the general public in National and EU institutions for 25 countries of Europe (percentage of respondents that tend to trust)

	NJ	*NP*	*NG*	*ECJ*	*EP*	*EC*
Mean	52%	36%	38%	50%	56%	52%
Min–Max	17–86%	13–71%	13–63%	33–73%	33–73%	30–70%
SD	19.3	17.2	13.7	11.2	10.5	10.4
Correlation						
NJ	1	0.85**	0.78**	0.68**	0.42*	0.39
NP		1	0.89**	0.78**	0.62**	0.58**
NG			1	0.80**	0.67**	0.66**
ECJ				1	0.86**	0.84**
EP					1	0.97**
EC						1

Notes

1. NJ: national judiciary, NP: national parliament, NG: national government, ECJ: European Court of Justice, EP: European Parliament and EC: European Commission

2. Correlation is significant: **at 0.01 level and *at 0.05 level (2-tailed)

2. Paired sample *T*-test of means on country level: means regarding *NG and NP*, *NJ and ECJ*, *NJ and EP*, *NJ and* EC and *ECJ and* EC do not differ significantly, while the other pairs differ (<0.01)

Source European Commission, Public Opinion, Eurobarometer Interactive

Trust in national institutions, data 06/2019 and trust in EU institutions, data 11/2019

At the country level, high trust nationally combines with a lower level of trust in the ECJ, and low trust nationally combines with higher trust in the ECJ (see Fig. 6.1a). Still, countries with high trust nationally, have more confidence in the ECJ than countries with low trust nationally. To illustrate: if trust in national justice is smaller than 50%, then the trust in the ECJ is higher than trust in national justice in 9 out of 12 countries, in 2 equal and only in one country substantially lower (Czechia). If trust is higher than 50%, in 12 out of 13 countries trust in the ECJ is lower than in the national courts (Belgium is the exception). Trust in the ECJ is higher in these countries than in the countries that have low trust in their judiciaries (57% tends to trust the ECJ vs 44%).

In Fig. 6.1 the trust in the three state powers is mapped for the national and the EU level. The logical consequence of the outcomes on trust discussed so far is that only for the judiciary there is a tipping point (at 50%), where higher trust in the ECJ turns into lower trust than nationally. For the other branches of government trust in the national institutions is nearly always lower than or equal to the trust in the EU institutions. These data are intriguing. National judiciaries command more trust than the other state powers in their political manifestations. As we saw in the previous section, this may have to do with the non-politicized nature of their judicial tasks that allows broad trust to develop among the population, but also with being embedded in an EU judicial system that from the top of the ECJ and the ECHR tries to promote and protect the independence and quality of the national judiciaries. This follows from their judgments but also from their (moral) leadership role in Europe.

Whether the trust of the population of a country in the ECJ is helpful in protecting judicial independence in countries with judiciaries that are under pressure from government and parliament, is an open question. In several of these countries the percentage of citizens that trust the ECJ falls below 50%, and that level of support may not sway government and parliament to implement unwelcome decisions of the ECJ. Nonetheless, the ECJ is likely to have a stabilizing influence on national judicial systems.

6.4 Trust and Respect of Independence

In this chapter the very high correlation of independence as perceived by citizens and their trust in the judiciary was discussed. In Chapter 3 the correlation between independence as perceived by judges and by citizens was examined. The connection between these concepts and respect

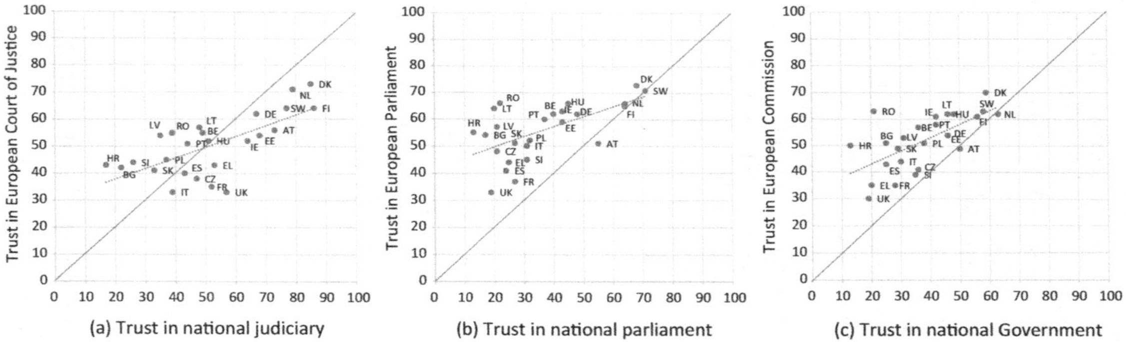

Fig. 6.1 Trust of citizens in national and EU institutions, percentage of respondents that tends to trust, average per country **a** National Judiciary and European Court of Justice, **b** National Parliament and European Parliament, and **c** National Government and European Commission (*Note* Trend line of 6.1(a): trust ECJ = 0.397** × trust NJ + 29.8, $N = 25$, $R^2 = 0.46$. 6.1(b): trust EP = 0.379** × trust NP + 42.0, $N = 25$, $R^2 = 0.38$. 6.1(c): trust EC = 0.503** × trust NG + 32.9, $N = 25$, $R^2 = 0.44$. *Source* European Commission, Public Opinion, Eurobarometer Interactive. Trust in national institutions, data 06/2019 and trust in EU institutions, data 11/2019)

for independence was not yet discussed. Table 6.5 gives the correlation between respect for independence by the main actors on the one hand and perceived independence and trust on the other hand.

While all correlations between variables at the national level are significant, respect for independence from parties and lawyers is particularly connected with judicial independence and trust. As such, this does not tell us anything about causality. However, respect for independence is based on the perceptions of judges, and it is likely that causality runs directly from their experience of respect for independence to their perceptions of independence. As to the connection between respect perceived by judges and perceived independence by citizens and their trust in the judiciary, causality is likely to run both ways. Parties, in particular, will be more respectful for judges, the more they are convinced of their independence and the more they trust them. At the same time, respect enhances independence and thereby trust.

Respect for independence by parliament and government is less strongly correlated with the perceptions of independence and trust, with the media taking a position in the middle. Respect and legitimacy of judges in the political field are less directly associated with the daily work of judges in their court rooms. Respect for independence by the other state powers has to do with matters of demarcation of responsibilities and resource allocation, as discussed in Chapter 5. The correlation of the

Table 6.5 Pearson correlations between independence and respect for independence as perceived by judges and independence and trust perceived by citizens

		Judges on	*Citizens on*		
		Independence	*Independence*	*Trust in Judiciary*	*Trust in ECJ*
Respect for independence by:	Parties	0.82**	0.79**	0.86**	0.60**
	Lawyers	0.88**	0.81**	0.84**	0.46*
	Parliament	0.62**	0.60**	0.66**	0.41
	Government	0.59**	0.53*	0.59**	0.40
	Trad. media	0.72**	0.71**	0.76**	0.58**

Notes

1. 22 countries
2. All variables are scores between 0–10, except trust in judiciary and ECJ which are % of respondents that tend to trust.

trust in the ECJ and the respect shown by the court users emphasizes the connectivity of the EU legal system.

References

Arnold, C., E.V. Sapir, and G. Zapryanova. 2012. Trust in the institutions of the European Union: A cross country examination. *European Integration Online Papers, Special Mini-Issue* 2: 16.

Coman, R. 2014. Quo vadis judicial reform? The quest for judicial independence in Central and Eastern Europe. *Europe-Asia Studies* 66 (6): 892–924.

Dekker, P., and J. den Ridder. 2020. Burgerperspectieven 2020/1. SCP.

GBAO. 2020. State of the State Courts, Survey analysis.

Grönlund, K., and M. Setälä. 2012. In honest officials we trust: Institutional confidence in Europe. *American Review of Public Administration* 42 (5): 523–542.

Papadopoulos, Y. 2013. *Democracy in crisis? Politics, Governance and Policy*. Cham: Palgrave Macmillan.

Sapignoli, M. (2018). Trust in justice in EU countries: Level of support and correlated factors. Paper prepared for 2018 EGPA Conference, Study Group XVIII on Justice and Court Administration.

Vaterrodt, J., M. Bohlen, and M. Sommer. 2018. Einstellung der Bevölkerung zum deutschen Justizsystem und zur Außergerichlichten Konfliktlösung; Roland Rechtsreport 2019, IfD Allensbach and Roland.

Warren, M.E. 1999. Democratic theory and trust. In *Democracy & trust*, ed. M.E. Warren, 1–21. Cambridge: Cambridge University Press.

CHAPTER 7

Judiciary in Democracy: Alignment and Disconnect

Abstract In this last Chapter, the consequences of differences in perceptions are examined. Two concepts are used: the lack of alignment and—more extreme—the disconnect between judiciary and society. Ranking countries by trust in the judiciary, in the lowest 20% there is a disconnect of judiciary and society, in the 20% around the median and in the highest 20% there is lack of alignment. Disconnect and lack of alignment seem to be self-perpetuating, as judges do not perceive the state of independence as problematic. Indications are that even a disconnect does not reduce the use of the civil courts, but that it leads citizens to avoid administrative law procedures. A disconnect weakens the position of the judiciary within the trias politica. This reinforces the complicated relationship between the judiciary and the other state powers. Where the other state powers see an increasing influence of the judiciary, the judiciary sees its own independence endangered. These perspectives clash. For the judiciary the way out is to focus on access to justice as an alternative perspective. By addressing the urgent legal needs of citizens, the judiciary has the potential to improve its alignment with society and its position within the trias politica.

Keywords Alignment · Disconnect · Judiciary · Democracy · Trias politica

F. van Dijk, *Perceptions of the Independence of Judges in Europe*,
https://doi.org/10.1007/978-3-030-63143-7_7

7.1 Definition of Lack of Alignment and Disconnect

In Chapter 3 it is shown that, while the perceptions of the independence of judiciary by relevant groups are correlated across countries, their perceptions differ in level. Who rates the judicial system on this crucial dimension, makes a huge difference. The perceptions by judges of their own independence are more positive than their perceptions of the independence of the judges in general in their country, in turn these perceptions are more positive than the perceptions of lawyers about judicial independence and these again are (much) more positive than the perceptions of the general public and that of companies. Also, level of education has an impact on perceptions with citizens with low education being less positive about judicial independence for medium and high levels of independence. While the data about court users is scarce and contradictory, it seems that experience lowers the perception of independence further. This is consistent with research for the US that suggests that for most people going to court is losing control over their situation, and that this loss of control as such leads to a negative experience (Benesh 2006). In addition it was shown in Chapter 3 that winning or losing plays a role, where losing is likely to get greater weight in the minds of people than winning, resulting on balance in a negative effect on perceived independence.

In Chapter 4 it is shown for a smaller set of countries that citizens who act as lay judges have perceptions about the independence of lay judges and of professional judges that are at the same level as the perceptions of professional judges. Their perceptions are much more positive than those of the highly educated general public. In the comparison of citizens as lay judges and as parties, judging versus being judged is likely to play an important role, and in the comparison of lay judges and the general public direct experience versus indirect information. Large differences in the perceptions of independence by judges including lay judges and the perceptions of the public in general and the public as parties reflect a lack of alignment between judiciary and society. A lack of alignment may turn into a disconnect when judges are (highly) positive about their independence and the public (highly) negative. In that case judges and those (potentially) being judged differ fundamentally on the actual realization of the core value of the judiciary. For citizens this is not (only) an abstract matter about the division of powers within the state, but about getting a fair trial. As discussed in Chapter 2, independence is a key aspect of procedural justice. Perceptions of independence, however, do not constitute the full picture.

Low levels of perceived judicial independence by the public may go together and may be exacerbated by lack of respect for independence by court users (parties, lawyers, prosecutors), the political system (parliament, government and media) and/or leaders of the judiciary (highest courts, governance bodies). Chapter 5 examines the perceptions of judges about the respect their independence receives from these groups. It is found that, according to the respondents, internal leaders respect the independence of the judges most, court users less so but still a lot, and the political system least. It is also shown that according to the judges respect for independence of the respective groups is based on different aspects of independence, related to the influence sphere of the respective actors. For instance, as to the parties, their respect is connected to corruption and inappropriate pressure, while for government and parliament the connection is with case load (budget) and the implementation of judgments that go against political interests. Combining perceptions about independence and respect for independence, a disconnect between judiciary and society is defined here as the combination of (1) positive perceptions of judicial independence by judges and negative perceptions by the general public, and (2) lack of respect for independence by the court users and the political system.

Chapter 6 incorporates trust in the framework. As discussed in Chapter 6, trust is a broad concept that can be applied to any function or organization. It is much less specific than independence, and precisely for that reason allows comparisons across institutions. For the judiciary it was shown that trust and independence are highly correlated to such an extent that trust in the judiciary equals trust in the independence of the judiciary. It was argued that independence or—more precisely—autonomy plays a role in government in general. Government consists of highly political policy making and more neutral policy implementation which is often executed by seperate organizations such as more or less autonomous agencies (see Chapter 2). For these latter organizations, impartiality and independence are important values, and they may even end up in court if they do not abide by these values. Trust in this public administration is likely to have a similar content as trust in the judiciary. For the political part of government and for parliament trust has necessarily another meaning, and, while it may contain neutral elements such as politicians handling crises competently, partisan aspects are part of it. For instance, politicians are expected by their constituencies to do what they promised to do at elections. This will be valued by their constituencies but not by other voters. As a consequence it is only logical that trust in government and parliament cannot reach the level of that of the judiciary, as long as the judiciary is not politicized itself. This is borne out by the data. In all well-established democracies trust in the judiciary is higher than in parliament and government. Thus, while at first sight equality of trust in the three powers of the state would seem desirable from a perspective of balance, equality cannot be the goal. For the judiciary an aspiration level would be to score higher than the public administration. In the mean across countries this is realized.

7.2 Alignment in Groups of Countries

Ordering the countries by means of one of the variables, trust in the (national) judiciary, three groups of countries are selected to examine the interaction of the perception variables at different levels of performance: the lowest 20%, the highest 20% and 20% symmetric around the median. Table 7.1 presents the results. In the lowest group trust in the judiciary is at the level of the other powers of the state, and is far below trust in public administration and regional and local public authorities. In the countries concerned trust in the judiciary at the EU-level is much higher than in the judiciary at the national level, but this does not seem to give the ECJ the trust that makes it politically risky for national government and parliament to ignore its judgments (see also Chapter 2). In these countries judges and lawyers are positive about judicial independence, but the general public is not. Neither are the parties. Citizens with a high education are even more negative about independence than citizens with a low education. This is remarkable. Citizens with a low education may be more susceptible to influence of the other state powers that in these countries show little respect for judicial independence. Not only respect by government and parliament is low, also in the court room respect by parties and lawyers is often not present.[1] This group of countries provides a clear case of the judiciary being disconnected from society. The situation

[1] The score in Table 7.1 for respect by court users in the lowest trust group corresponds to 57% of the responding judges (strongly) agreeing that their independence is respected, 16% disagreeing and 27% is uncertain.

Table 7.1 Trust, perceived independence and respect for independence for three groups of countries

	Lowest trust	*Middle trust*	*Highest trust*
Trust by general public (% that tends to trust) in:			
National judiciary	26.6%	49.6%	80%
Average parliament and government	24.2%	33.7%	60.8%
Average public administration and regional/local authorities	37.9%	52.1%	71.0%
European Court of Justice	44.8%	46.8%	65.6%
Perceived judicial independence (score 0–10) by:			
Judges (about independence of all judges)	7.1	8.0	9.1
Lawyers	5.9	6.0	8.0
General public	3.9	5.5	7.3
General public high education	3.8	5.6	7.6
General public low education	4.3	5.2	6.4
Parties	3.6	5.2	6.8
Respect for judicial independence perceived by judges (score 0–10) of:			
Court users (average parties and lawyers)	6.5	7.4	8.6
Political system (average parliament, government and media)	5.2	5.8	7.5
Court management	7.7	8.2	8.9

Notes
Lowest 20%: BG, HR, LT, SK, SL
Middle 20%: BE, CZ, EL, HU, LT
Highest 20%: AT, DK, FI, NL, SW

of these countries seems to be stable in a negative equilibrium, as there are no strong forces that pull towards judicial independence.

At the other end of the spectrum, nearly all variables point to a stable equilibrium as well, but then at a high level of trust and independence. In terms of trust, the courts outperform not only the other state powers but also the less-political public sector institutions. In addition, the link with the EU is relatively strong. Even if a government would be tempted to ignore judgments of the ECJ, this would likely meet resistance from within society, and could be risky for the government. Perceptions of independence by the respective groups are all positive. However, the perceptions of independence by parties and citizens with a low education are not as positive as the other outcomes would lead to expect. As a result, also in these countries the difference between judges and the general public and, in particular, the part that has little education is large. Thus, even the best performing judiciaries are not aligned with society. While the judiciary plays its role in a capable manner, its high self-esteem may cause it to be complacent, and as a result not deeply interested in the court users or the developments society is undergoing. This complacency shows in the lack of court user surveys (only two of the five countries in this group conduct such surveys) and, for instance, slow adaptation to digital and on-line communication, as a result of which courts also in these countries were cornered by the COVID 19 pandemic (ELI 2020).

In the middle, there is a diverse range of countries that seem to be in a less stable situation. Trust in the judiciary is well above trust in the other two branches of government, but just falls short of the public administration, and it is in an absolute sense low. The link with the European level is weak, and does not differ much from the lowest group. Perceived independence by citizens with low education and parties is only marginally positive, and differs starkly from the views of the judges. Respect for independence by the political system is low. These countries are likely to be evolving, either positively or negatively. Hungary and, before the detrimental reforms, Poland are cases in point of negative evolution, while Lithuania shows a positive evolution.

Figure 7.1a and b depict the essential data for all countries individually. If a difference smaller than 20% in perceived independence by judges and public is required for a judiciary to be aligned with society (see the dashed line in Fig. 7.1a), preciously few judiciaries live up to that standard. A combination of positive perceptions by judges and negative perceptions by the public occurs frequently. This happens in 9 countries.[2] In addition to the countries in the lowest 20% group, this occurs in Italy, Portugal, Spain and Romania. Figure 7.1b addresses respect for independence, and exhibits results for two actors, one from the category of court users (parties) and the other from the political system (parliament). The scores reflect the percentages of judges that feel their independence is (not) respected. It is to some extent arbitrary at which score the independence of the judiciary is seen to be not respected anymore. In the figure demarcation lines are drawn at a score of 7, roughly corresponding with

[2] Positive: the score is larger than 5, Negative: the score is smaller than 5. The smallest difference between a positive score by judges and a negative score by citizens is 23% (1.5 point).

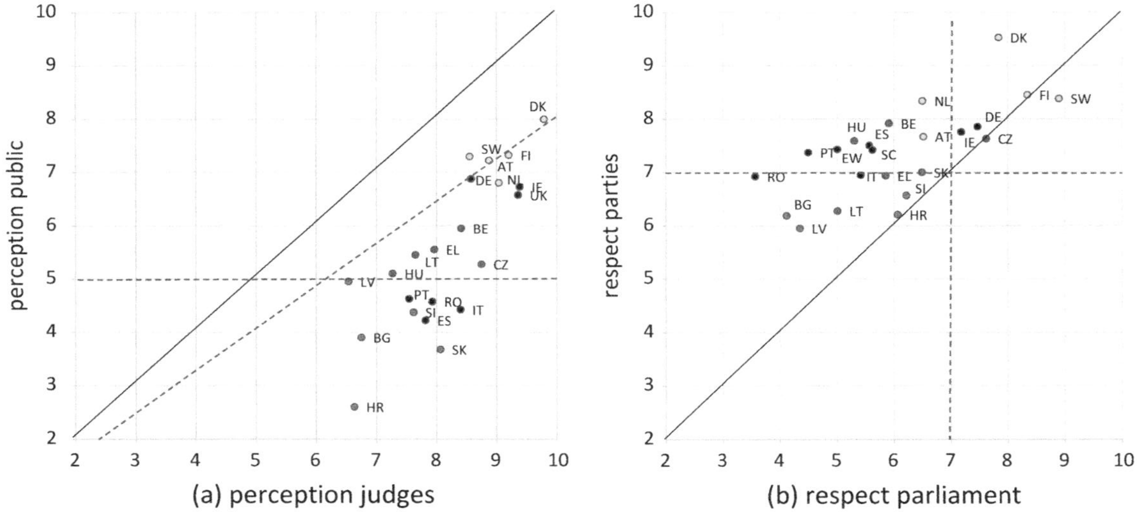

Fig. 7.1 Alignment of judiciary and society, average scores per country **a** Perception of independence by judges and public. **b** Respect for independence by parliament and parties to lawsuits. Red dots: lowest 20% of trust in judiciary, blue: 20% around the median and yellow: highest 20% (*Note* See list of country abbreviations at the end of Chapter 3) (Color figure online)

70% of the judges feeling respected. Using this criterion, few countries are fully in the clear, in particular with regard to respect from parliament.

7.3 Causes of Disconnect and Lack of Alignment

Can disconnect and lack of alignment be attributed to general causes? Two scenarios were suggested in Chapter 3. The alternative storylines were—briefly summarized—either the judiciary being overly confident or society overly critical. To review the evidence collected so far, in Chapter 3 the comparison of citizens and companies with and without experience with disputes at the courts was examined. For citizens the data show a lower appreciation of independence by citizens with than without experience. This does not bode well for the judiciary. However, it was also shown that views become more extreme, suggesting in particular that parties that lose their cases tend to have a (more) negative appreciation of independence. In combination with the general argument that going to court is not a positive experience as parties have to surrender control, it seems that the perceptions of the parties are overly negative. In Chapter 4 it was concluded that lay judges have similar perceptions about independence as professional judges. Albeit for a relatively small number of countries, the perceptions of lay judges give credence to the perceptions of judges.

From the data about the respect for independence it can be concluded that in the mean a large majority of judges feels their independence respected by the court users (see Fig. 7.1b for the parties to lawsuits). This as well as the respect for independence by court leaders is consistent with the positive perception of independence by judges. Judges experience less respect by the political system including the media. Thus, at system level there are more tensions than at the day-to-day work in the courts. The opinion of the general public is likely to be affected by media and politics. In particular if judges focus on their daily work as they are prone to do and which is where independence eventually materializes, they have the arguments on their side to be more positive about judicial independence than the general public. To conclude, judiciary and society are generally not aligned and in several countries there is an outright disconnect, but the judiciary is substantially more independent that the general public realizes. We conclude that both story lines are needed to explain the observed differences, but the relative contribution of both is difficult to assess.

7.4 Consequences of Disconnect and Lack of Alignment

Disconnect and lack of alignment may reduce the willingness of parties to bring cases to court. One would expect that in these circumstances plaintiffs in disputes more often either give up their claims altogether or try to find alternatives that are more trustworthy. Of course, they would need to convince defendants to agree with such a course. This is often difficult to achieve. At the other end of the spectrum, it is likely that independent courts that are not swayed by specific interests of any kind, are more consistent in their interpretation of the law, and their judgments can be predicted accurately. Therefore, it would be relatively easy to convince defendants to negotiate out of court and to settle, and there would be no reason to go to court.

The most relevant type of case to examine here are civil cases, as these cases leave choice to the parties and have some homogeneity across jurisdictions. To give a first impression of the data, as gathered by CEPEJ, the countries in the 20% lowest group of trust have 2.9 civil litigious cases per 100 inhabitants, and the highest group 0.68 civil cases.[3] It seems that in the countries that experience a disconnect people go to court abundantly, despite their misgivings about the independence of the judiciary. The same phenomenon has been observed for Russia (Hendley 2013). These figures do not prove, of course, that a disconnect leads to high case load, as many other variables play a role. Other factors such as disposition time and availability of alternatives, but also cultural factors like conflict handling behaviour need to be controlled for. For the present analysis it has to suffice that a disconnect does not dominate the actual use of the civil courts. The data of CEPEJ on administrative law show an inverted pattern with 0.22 cases per 100 inhabitants for the 20% lowest group versus 0.76 cases for the 20% highest bracket.[4] This suggests that in these countries people avoid litigating against the state. However, the scope of administrative law differs among countries, and an in-depth analysis is needed before firm conclusions can be drawn. That there are issues in administrative law or more in general with cases against government, is shown in the latest judges survey of the ENCJ (2019). The survey

[3] CEPEJ (2018, Fig. 5.5) (no data on Bulgaria).

[4] CEPEJ (2018, Fig. 5.23).

includes the statement that judgments that went against the interests of the government were usually implemented/enforced in the country of the respondent. In the lowest bracket of trust 23% does not agree with the statement and 52% is not sure, while in the 20% highest bracket 12% does not agree and 31% is not sure.[5] Thus, when one wins a case against the government, the chances that the government will honour the judgment are much lower in the former than in the latter countries. This reduces the incentive to go to court. This issue is broader than the lowest bracket, as in the middle group these percentages were 25% and 43%.

At the system level, lack of alignment and disconnect, in particular, weaken the position of the judiciary in the trias politica, and this may have diverse consequences ranging from insufficient allocation of resources, politicized appointments to governance bodies of the judiciary, taking tasks away from the judiciary and, as just noted, refusal by government to implement judgments. A disconnect may also make it easier for governments to succeed in policies towards illiberal democracy, including reforms of judiciaries to bring them under the control of government or parliament. After all, governments do not have to fear large popular support for the judiciary and its independence. In the multi-level governance system of the EU, resistance will come from the EU institutions and currently, in particular, from the ECJ that, as was shown, is trusted more than national judiciaries, but probably not enough to have decisive influence.

A disconnect but also a milder lack of alignment is likely to be self-perpetuating, as judiciaries do not see much need for connection with society, accountability, change and innovation, while society gets more frustrated by the lack thereof. To illustrate diverging sense of urgency, in the recent surveys among judges and lawyers it is found, for instance, that on the question whether judicial corruption is effectively addressed by the judicial authorities in the respondent's country a large difference exists between what judges and what lawyers answer.[6] For the 20% lowest bracket of trust, 12% of judges and 53% of lawyers give a negative answer and for the 20% highest bracket 2% of judges and 14% of lawyers. This does not show much recognition among judges of the urgency of change seen by lawyers, in particular, in the lowest 20% bracket.

[5] ENCJ (2019, Fig. 10).

[6] ENCJ (2019, Fig. 34) and ENCJ/CCBE (2019, Fig. 20).

7.5 Judiciary in a Democracy

An important component of the lack of alignment and disconnect of the judiciary with society is the complicated relationship between the state powers. As discussed, many judges feel that their independence is not respected. The background of the tensions between the branches of government can be found in long term developments. The judiciary operates on the one hand at the micro level of the day to day adjudication of the many disputes involving citizens and/or businesses, and on the other hand at the macro level of fundamental decisions that affect government, its responsibilities and the boundaries it cannot transgress. Because of these fundamental decisions, the way the judiciary is perceived and treated by the other state powers cannot be separated from the changes democracies in Europe are going through in their relation with the judiciary. Depending on the trend one focusses on, there are several perspectives on the development of European democracies. From a *political* perspective, the worldwide trend of the gradually increasing influence of the courts on political decision-making, so-called 'judicialization', is particularly relevant. This long-term trend is generally interpreted as an ongoing transfer of power from the organs of representative democracy to judiciaries (see e.g. the review by Hirschl 2009). The increasing reach of constitutional courts is an important component of this trend, but also the regular administrative and civil courts have a growing impact on government policies. One of the multiple causes is the increasing importance of fundamental rights and freedoms and law in general. Constitutional democracy replaces popular democracy (Mény and Surel 2002): political decisions are subject to judicial review and the leeway of politicians is reduced. The development of the European Union with its far reaching regulations and creation of independent European and national regulators, is a major factor. As national judges enforce European law and in that sense can not only rhetorically be called European judges,[7] the national judiciaries are seen as reducing the degrees of freedom of national politics. While politicians have committed themselves earlier to EU rules and regulations, the judiciary holds them to that commitment. Judicialization is part of a broader trend of "the rise of the unelected" (Vibert 2007). The agencification that was briefly discussed in Chapter 2 is part of this

[7] E.g., "National judges are European judges and they oversee the application of EU law". Vice-president of the EC, Timmermans, on Twitter 21 February 2019.

trend (Verhoest 2017). The ubiquitous creation of independent national regulators goes well beyond granting autonomy to agencies that remain under the direction of ministers. Their formal safeguards of independence are similar to those of the judiciary (OECD 2016), and they derive much of their position and power from the judiciary (OECD 2017). Another example of declining influence of national politicians is the position of the national Central Banks that in as far as community tasks (such as monetary policy) are concerned, are independent. Their independence has been arranged in a detailed manner, and forbids, for instance, the giving of instructions to the governors of the Bank. Recourse to a court is often possible if a Bank feels its independence is breached. The president of a national Central Bank can, for instance, appeal against his/her dismissal to the ECJ, while other members of decisions making bodies can address a national court (ECB 2018).

These developments are experienced by politicians as a threat to representative democracy. In particular, populist politicians who oppose Europeanization regularly express fear of rule by judges (using terms such as government of judges, juristocracy, courtocracy, dikastocracy and kritocracy), but discomfort about loss of influence to the judiciary is broader among politicians than only the populist right and left. This judicialization happens at a time when representative democracy is under internal pressures, for instance due to the changing nature of political parties and their leadership (Papadopoulos 2013). In the context of this book, it should be noted that judicialization presupposes that the judiciary is 'reasonably independent' (Hirschl 2009, p 130). This brings us to the second perspective.

In a *rule of law* perspective, one can see the judiciary and in particular its independence under threat from politicians who have in many ways a strong grip on the judiciary and who do not want to relinquish that grip. Where this grip was relinquished in the past, politicians often yearn to get it back. If one examines the Justice Scoreboard of the EC and the indicators of independence and accountability of the ECNJ, the impression one gets of the judiciary is a conglomerate of judges that is in many respects dependent on the other state powers, even in some countries for the day to day management of the courts (EC 2020; ENCJ 2020; van Dijk and Vos 2018). Even in countries in which the judiciary is an autonomous organization, it is often heavily dependent on government and parliament for budget and for appointments to leadership positions, for instance, at Councils for the Judiciary (e.g. Torres Pérez 2019 on Spain). Pressure on the judiciary has also a public communication component: in the media the critique of lack of democratic legitimacy is often levelled against the judiciary when judgments are not welcome. In Central and Eastern European countries at the accession to the Union the independence of the judiciary was often well arranged, and this shows in the indicators of the ENCJ, mentioned above. These judiciaries have stronger formal safeguards than most countries in Western Europe that traditionally operate on the basis of mutual trust and respect. In several of the countries of Central and Eastern Europe politicians try to recapture the grip that they relinquished (Coman 2014; Kovács and Scheppele 2018; Sterk and van Dijk 2019). Their authoritarian leaders call the resulting form of government illiberal democracy. Especially in these countries, judiciaries feel threatened. In other countries there is often a feeling within the judiciary of being kept short by the other state powers, also literally in terms of caseloads and budgets. The judiciaries of Europe brace themselves against an often combined power block of government and parliament to maintain their independence.

In a *access to justice* perspective, the focus is on the day-to-day plight of ordinary people and businesses seeking justice. In all countries a substantial part of their legal needs are not met (for a brief summary of the extensive literature see OECD/WJP). If disputes have been resolved by settlement or adjudication, many believe this resolution was not achieved in a fair manner. In addition, in many judiciaries (larger) court cases take a long time, are costly and are administratively complicated, partly due to lagging ICT-systems. In this perspective the judiciary is an important part of conflict resolution chains which it ideally guides by a clear and uniform application of the law. As a result people would not have to go to court in most cases. Procedural justice plays, next to access to justice, a central role in this approach: not only in cases of citizens against government but in all party configurations. Procedural justice requires judges in each case to be independent and to convey this to the parties and, if the case is of sufficient interest, to the media and society in general.

Obviously, the first two perspectives collide, leading at best to misunderstandings between politicians who only see an empowered judiciary that they do not consider in need of strengthening further, and a judiciary that sees its—often already limited—independence under threat by reform proposals and by mundane issues like insufficient budgets. At its worst this leads to power struggles that spill over to the EU level. Government and parliament on the one side and the judiciary on the other side feel threatened by each other. The relatively low scores on respect for judicial independence by the political system, as perceived by the judiciary, testify to this from the perspective of the judiciary. In this context, a beauty contest about who is trusted the most, is not helpful and, as was discussed in Chapter 6, beside the point. One may wonder what is the way out of this situation.

In this Chapter the conclusion was reached that judiciaries are characterized by a lack of alignment or even a disconnect with society. This shows in particular in very diverse views of judges and citizens about judicial independence, and in case of a disconnect by positive perceptions of independence by judges and negative perceptions by citizens, as well as low respect of independence by the court users and the political system. Lack of alignment and disconnect are to some extent a reflection of the above collision. Both are also connected to lack of knowledge in society about the judiciary which was shown by the much more positive perceptions of independence by knowledgeable lay judges than by ordinary (even highly educated) citizens. Judiciaries perform better than the public is aware of. Still, these reasons cannot fill the whole gap in perceptions between judges and the rest of society. Within the judiciary, the reason must be sought in a generally weak orientation on the court users. While many courts perform well in this respect by sticking to their core values, feedback mechanisms are hardly anywhere established. In Chapter 3 the weak court user orientation that speaks from the scarcity of court user surveys was discussed. Guaranteeing that people get real access to justice, irrespective of their background and that of the other parties in judicial proceedings, is not at the forefront in most courts. This affects the appreciation of the public for the courts and can easily lead to a negative perception of independence and low trust. In addition, it weakens the position of the judiciary in the debate with politicians, as judges cannot count on much support from the population.

Therefore, the third perspective of access to justice is important for society and judiciary. This perspective as such is likely to be less controversial than the other perspectives, despite its reliance on the rule of law in every-day cases. It requires constructive co-operation within conflict resolution chains in order to empower people to resolve disputes themselves on the basis of adequate information or assistance, and, secondary, to unburden the courts of cases that are trivial from a legal point of view.

To let such chains work smoothly, courts have to be consistent and fast. And they must be truly independent, and make sure that the parties and everybody else involved are fully aware of that. In this way, the judiciary will better connect with society, and it will, indirectly, promote its independence. Building broad public support by promoting and guaranteeing access to justice, including fair trial, is not only essential to maintain the authority of the judge in the court room, but also to maintain the position of the judiciary in the political arena.

However, the positive perception of their independence by most judges that emerged from the surveys, leads inadvertently to a low urgency to improve performance and image. This rather myopic attitude in a further broad minded group of professionals is one of the striking characteristics of the judiciary (see for the US Rottman and Tomkins 1999). As mentioned already, it would be helpful if judges became more interested in the experiences of the court users, in particular with regard to fundamental issues as independence and impartiality. A far sighted approach would to be to try and bring the perceptions of the court users and citizens in general together with those of the judges. Exactly in view of the importance of avoiding the appearance of dependence and partiality, the reduction of differences in perceptions is advisable, even if this means adjusting the perceptions of the judges downward.

Returning to the interaction of the powers of the state, it was suggested earlier in this Chapter, based on the data presented, that the outcome may or may not be that the judiciary of a country is in a stable equilibrium. A stable equilibrium seems to occur at a high or at a low level of—in combination—perceived independence, respect for independence and trust in the judiciary. If a stable system is out of equilibrium for instance due to temporary negative events such as a deep economic crisis or positive events such as large external support, it will return after some time to its former equilibrium. The judiciaries that were classified as stable are not easy to get permanently out of balance. When in a positive balance, this is a desirable characteristic, but in a negative equilibrium, this is not. A disconnect between judiciary and society, that characterizes a negative equilibrium, is hard to overcome. In-between there are countries of which the powers of the state do not seem to be in equilibrium. Large improvements and large deteriorations in the rule of law occur and may even alternate. Poland and Hungary are examples of countries in which political leaders were able to change the judicial institutions radically, despite elaborate legal safeguards and despite being embedded in the European

Union. These upheavals follow from the clash of perspectives that was discussed above. A long term defence against such upheavals is a sharp focus of the judiciary on delivering justice for the population, and to build popular support.

References

Benesh, S.C. 2006. Understanding public confidence in American courts. *Journal of Politics* 68 (3): 697–707.

CEPEJ. 2018. European judicial systems: Efficiency and quality. CEPEJ Studies No 23.

Coman, R. 2014. Quo vadis judicial reform? The quest for judicial independence in Central and Eastern Europe. *Europe-Asia Studies* 66 (6): 892–924.

ELI. 2020. ELI Webinar on Back to Normal: Checks and Balances (Legislator/Judiciary). https://www.europeanlawinstitute.eu/news-events/news-contd/news/eli-webinar-on-back-to-normal-checks-and-balances-legislatorjudiciary.

ENCJ. 2019. Independence and accountability of the judiciary: ENCJ Survey on the independence of judges 2019. encj.eu.

ENCJ. 2020. Independence, accountability and quality of the judiciary: Measuring for improvement. ENCJ Report 2019–2020. www.encj.eu.

ENCJ and CCBE. 2019. Independence and accountability of the judiciary: ENCJ/CCBE Survey among lawyers on the independence of judges 2019. www.encj.eu.

European Central Bank. 2018. ECB convergence report. ecb.europa.eu.

European Commission. 2020. 2020 EU Justice Scoreboard.

Hendley, K. 2013. The puzzling non-consequences of societal distrust of courts: Explaining the use of Russian courts. *Cornell International Law Journal* 45: 517–567.

Hirschl, R. 2009. The judicialization of politics. In *The Oxford Handbook of Law and Politics*, ed. G.D. Caldeira, R.D. Keleman and K.E. Whittington. New York: Oxford University Press.

Kovács, K., and K. Scheppele. 2018. The fragility of an independent judiciary: Lessons from Hungary and Poland—And the European Union. *Communist and Post-Communist Studies* 51: 189–200.

Mény, Y., and Y. Surel. 2002. *Democracies and the populist challenge*. Cham: Palgrave Macmillan.

OECD. 2016.*Being an independent regulator; The governance of regulators*. OECD Publishing.

OECD. 2017. The regulator and his judge(s); Conference organised in cooperation with the OECD Network of Economic Regulators.

OECD/WJP (x). Building a business case for access to justice. An OECD White Paper in collaboration with the World Justice Project.

Papadopoulos, Y. 2013. *Democracy in crisis? Politics, Governance and Policy*. Cham: Palgrave Macmillan.

Rottman, D.B., and A.J. Tomkins. 1999. Public trust and confidence in the courts: What public opinion surveys mean to judges. *Court Review* 36 (3): 24–31.

Sterk, K., and F. van Dijk. 2019. Protecting the Independence of National Councils of the Judiciary on the EU Level, VerfBlog, 17 September. https://verfassungsblog.de/protecting-the-independence-of-national-councils-of-the-judiciary-on-the-eu-level/arnold.

Torres Pérez, A. 2019. Judicial self-government and judicial independence: The political capture of the general council of the judiciary in Spain. *German Law Journal* 19 (7): 1769–1800.

van Dijk, F., and G. Vos. 2018. A method for assessment of the independence and accountability of the judiciary. *Special Issue, International Journal of Court Administration* 9 (3): 1–21.

Verhoest, K. 2017. Agentification. In *The Palgrave Handbook of Public Administration and Management in Europe*, ed. E. Ongaro and S. van Thiel, 327–346. Basingstoke: Palgrave Macmillan.

Vibert, F. 2007. *The rise of the unelected: Democracy and the new separation of powers*. Cambridge: Cambridge University Press.

Index

A

Access to justice, 105–107
Administrative law, 101
Agencification, 20, 103
Alignment, 2–5, 22, 24, 48, 94, 99–103, 106
Autonomy, 20, 21, 95, 104

B

Brexit, 67, 80, 83
Budget, 66, 95, 104, 105
  mechanism, 106

C

Case load, 70–72, 95, 101
Central Bank, 87, 104
CEPEJ, 12, 13, 43, 54, 101
Civil law, 54
Companies, 3, 5, 23, 30, 32, 33, 35, 41, 42, 44–48, 78, 79, 94, 100
Confidence, 14–18, 43, 82, 83, 89
Constitution, 20, 22
Constitutional court, 66, 68, 69, 73, 103
Corruption, 10, 70, 71, 95, 102
Council for the judiciary, 54, 74
Council of Bars and Law Societies of Europe (CCBE), 5, 30, 31, 102
Court user survey, 6, 12, 31, 42, 43, 46, 47, 98, 106
Criminal law, 19

D

Democracy, 3, 6, 11, 13, 18, 67, 80, 82, 96, 102–105
Disconnect, 2, 5, 62, 94, 95, 100–103, 106, 107
Distrust, 15, 49, 85

E

Education, 18, 37–40, 47, 48, 58, 94, 96–98
Enemies of the people, 23, 67, 82
Equilibrium, 6, 22, 97, 107
Europe, 3, 5, 8, 14, 16, 22, 30, 32, 33, 40, 42, 82, 89, 103, 105
  Central, 80, 105
  Eastern, 3, 40, 105

F. van Dijk, *Perceptions of the Independence of Judges in Europe*,
https://doi.org/10.1007/978-3-030-63143-7

European Commission (EC), 4, 5, 16, 17, 21, 30, 31, 37, 39–42, 67, 78–81, 84, 86–88, 90, 103, 104
European Court of Human Rights (ECHR), 8, 11, 21, 87, 89
European Court of Justice (ECJ), 21, 24, 78, 87–92, 96, 97, 102, 104
European Network of Councils for the judiciary (ENCJ), 9, 16, 30, 31, 33, 34, 55, 57, 67, 68, 70, 101, 102, 104, 105
European Parliament (EP), 81, 87, 88, 90

G
Government, 2–5, 15, 17, 19, 20, 23, 24, 66–72, 74, 80–83, 85–91, 95–97, 101–105
  multi level, 102

H
Hierarchy, 21, 54, 68
Hungary, 3, 20, 35, 36, 39, 41, 44, 67, 98, 107

I
Impartiality, 11, 12, 15, 17, 18, 31, 43, 46, 47, 78, 85, 95, 107
Incentive, 2, 19, 66, 102
Independence, 1–6, 8–24, 30, 32–41, 43–49, 54, 56, 58–62, 66, 68–72, 74, 78, 79, 85, 86, 91, 94–98, 100–102, 104–107
  de facto, 3, 14, 18
  de iure, 9, 18, 20
  perceived, 1, 4, 5, 10, 15, 18, 22, 24, 38, 43, 44, 48, 59, 60, 69, 71, 72, 78, 79, 81, 89, 91, 94, 97, 107
Ivory tower, 24, 48

J
Judge
  appointment, 2, 9, 34
  election, 22
  promotion, 34, 70, 72
Judges association, 69
Judicial decision, 37, 70
  enforcement, 19
  implementation, 12, 23, 67
Judicialization, 103, 104
Judicial review, 85, 103
Juristocracy, 104
Juror, 17, 43

L
Lawyer, 2–5, 10, 13, 14, 16, 23, 30–33, 35–39, 42, 44, 47–49, 54, 66, 68, 69, 71, 72, 91, 94, 96, 97, 102
Lay judge, 5, 14, 16, 23, 30, 31, 49, 54–62, 86, 94, 100
Legal problem, 9
Legislation, 21, 67
Legitimacy, 2, 14–17, 21, 22, 66, 67, 72, 74, 91, 105
Legitimation, 19
Local and regional authorities, 83, 85, 86, 96, 97

M
Media, 2–4, 10, 12, 13, 23, 24, 39, 49, 67, 68, 70, 72, 82, 91, 95, 97, 100, 105
  social media, 3, 13, 48, 67–69, 72
  traditional media, 13, 66, 68, 69, 72
Mixed panels, 55, 56, 59, 61
Mixed teams, 59, 61

N
Need for change, 24, 25

O

Obligation, 8, 15, 16

P

Parliament, 2–5, 19, 23, 24, 66–72, 80–83, 85, 86, 89, 91, 95–100, 102, 104–106
- European (EP), 81, 87, 88, 90
- national (NP), 80, 87, 88, 90

Perception, 3–5, 9–11, 13, 14, 17, 18, 20, 21, 23, 24, 30–33, 35–37, 39–44, 46–49, 54, 56–58, 61, 62, 66, 68, 86, 91, 94–96, 98, 100, 106, 107
- formation of, 12
- of independence, 3, 4, 12, 13, 18, 36–38, 41, 43, 56, 57, 59, 78, 79, 91, 94, 95, 97, 99, 100, 106

Poland, 3, 14, 20, 21, 31, 41, 55, 57, 58, 61, 67, 74, 79, 83, 86, 98, 107

Police, 19, 83

Policy, 20, 21, 85, 95, 102–104
- development, 85
- implementation, 85, 95

Political science, 20

President of the court, 66, 68

Pressure, 2, 8–11, 14, 23, 59, 70–72, 89, 95, 104, 105

Procedural justice, 12, 17, 18, 44, 95, 105

Public administration, 83, 85, 86, 95–98

Public prosecutor, 66

R

Regulation, 20, 103

Reputation, 20

Rule of law, 2, 3, 18, 40, 86, 87, 106, 107

S

State courts, 17, 24, 40, 42, 43, 82

State powers, 2–6, 13, 18, 19, 21, 25, 68, 78, 80, 81, 87, 89, 91, 96, 97, 103–105

Support, 2, 12, 15, 17, 19, 20, 23, 39, 40, 67, 89, 102, 106, 107

Supreme court, 23, 66–72, 82

Survey, 3–6, 12, 13, 16–18, 23, 30, 31, 33–36, 39–44, 47, 54–57, 59–61, 66, 68, 70, 71, 78–80, 82, 83, 86, 87, 98, 101, 107

T

Trias politica, 19, 102

Trust
- diffuse, 15, 16
- dispositional, 15–18, 86
- institutional, 15, 86
- personal, 15
- specific, 15, 86

Trustworthiness, 12, 15–17, 22

U

United States (US), 9, 12, 14, 16, 17, 24, 39, 40, 42, 43, 47, 82, 83, 94, 107